Assessment

A Framework for Teachers

Assessment

A Framework for Teachers

Ruth Sutton

with illustrations by Jim Whittaker

First published 1991 by the NFER-Nelson Publishing Company

Reprinted 1992, 1994 and 1995
by Routledge
11 New Fetter Lane, London EC4P 4EE

© 1991 Ruth Sutton

Typeset by David John Services Ltd, Maidenhead, Berkshire
Printed and bound in Great Britain by
Biddles Ltd, Guildford and King's Lynn

British Library Cataloguing in Publication Data
A catalogue record for this book is available from the British Library

Library of Congress Cataloguing in Publication Data
A catalogue record for this book is available from the Library of Congress

ISBN 0-415-08490-3

Contents

List of Figures and Illustrations

A Guide to the Terminology

Chapter One is designed to explain in detail some of the 'jargon' of assessment. Other than that, the terminology mainly derives from the National Curriculum structure itself. For those of you unfamiliar with this structure, some explanation here will help. All these terms are explored in greater depth throughout the book.

Core and Foundation Subject. The National Curriculum categorizes learning into subject areas. Of these, mathematics, science and English are described as *core* subjects. In addition, seven *foundation* subjects are presented. These are technology, history, geography, art, music, physical education, and modern foreign languages. Religious education is not subject to National Curriculum assessment, but is required for all pupils. Currently, modern foreign languages are not required for pupils before the age of 11 years, and children may be allowed to choose at the age of 14 years between history and geography, and between art and music.

Year Groups. The National Curriculum uses a new and simplified way of describing the year groups of pupils. What used to be commonly called the 'Middle Infant' Year, with children around 6 years of age is now called Year One, and so on up the age range. 'Top Junior' becomes Year Six, and students in their final year of compulsory schooling at age 16 years are in Year Eleven. Many schools have now adopted this system.

Key Stages. Compulsory schooling from age 5 to 16 years is now divided into four Key Stages:

1. *Key Stage One*: Reception, Year One and Two;
2. *Key Stage Two*: Years Three, Four, Five and Six;
3. *Key Stage Three*: Years Seven, Eight and Nine; and
4. *Key Stage Four*: Years Ten and Eleven.

Programmes of Study. These describe what children are to be taught, in each subject area, at each key stage. They are statutory, and all children are entitled to have the programmes of study presented to them. The governing body is legally responsible for ensuring this entitlement.

National Curriculum Levels. There are ten levels, as defined by the Task Group on Assessment and Testing (TGAT) in 1987. These levels are based on what children would normally be expected to do, know and understand at different ages. The levels as described in each subject area, therefore, are *norm-based.*

Attainment Targets (ATs). These are the description of what children are expected to have learned as they work through the programmes of study. They divide the subject into its various components to allow us to describe learning quite specifically. Almost all attainment targets are described at all levels. Attainment targets describe the *output* of the National Curriculum: programmes of study describe the input of the National Curriculum. Obviously, therefore, these are very closely connected.

Statements of Attainment. Many of the attainment targets described at levels are subdivided into smaller assessment criteria, known as statements of attainment. These are designed to give teachers a clearer idea of what to look for in a child's learning as they monitor their progress. Pupils can find these helpful too, to show what they are aiming for, but they will often need help to understand the language used.

Profile Components. These are clumps of attainment targets taken together to simplify how we report children's learning to parents and others. In some cases, the profile component contains one attainment target, and in others, more than one. In English, there are three profile components – Speaking and Listening, Reading, and Writing. Of these the first two have one attainment target each, but the third, Writing, has three to describe different aspects of a child's written work.

Records of Achievement. This term is used by the Department of Education and Science to describe the way schools describe and report an individual child's learning and development, both within the

National Curriculum and beyond. The record of achievement is a way of bringing together information about a child that allows the uniqueness of the child or young person to show through. National Curriculum reporting is therefore just a part of the overall picture, reflecting the fact the National Curriculum itself is only a part of the child's overall experience of education.

Standard Assessment Task (SAT). This is specially devised to provide a common assessment experience for all pupils at or near the end of the key stage. These tasks will not cover all the attainment targets in all areas, as Teacher Assessment will.

Teacher Assessment (TA). The continual process by which teachers monitor and record children's National Curriculum levels for each attainment target, completed by the end of the key stage.

Introduction

My aim is to present ways of thinking about assessment that have been developing in my head for several years, constantly honed and sharpened by involvement with real teachers in real schools. The book offers some clarification, hopefully, and some ideas, but many questions too—to which there are no definitive answers. I have tried to keep it simple, brief and readable by anyone looking for a quick dive in to what sometimes seems a rather muddy pond. If you are still interested by the end of it, there are some more books suggested for further reading.

My thanks are due to countless teachers who have shared their experience and ideas with me, and to colleagues with whom I have worked and trained and traded information, materials and strategies. Among them I am particulary indebted to David Garforth, Steve Munby, John Turner and Jacky West. Thanks to Jim Whittaker for the fun and creativity of his cartoons, and especially to Mary McSherry, without whose constant support and patient deciphering of my scrawl this book would not have happened.

Chapter One:
The Framework of Ideas

'Promoting children's learning is a principal aim of schools. Assessment lies at the heart of this process. It can provide a framework in which educational objectives may be set, and pupils' progress charted and expressed. It can yield a basis for planning the next educational steps in response to children's needs. By facilitating dialogue between teachers, it can enhance professional skills and help the school as a whole to strengthen learning across the curriculum and throughout its age range.'

(Report of the Task Group on Assessment and Testing)

It is worth noting, right from the start, that assessment is a human process, conducted by and with human beings, and subject inevitably to the frailties of human judgement. However crisp and objective we might try to make it, and however neatly quantifiable may be our 'results', assessment is closer to an art than a science. It is, after all, an exercise in human communication.

This said, the fact remains that assessment of children's learning and progress is central to effective teaching and learning. Our reactions to it are rarely neutral: they have been affected by our own previous experience as pupils, and by our involvement with the educational progress of our own children. As teachers, in recent years, the task of assessing has become a greater part of our professional activity; the responsibility for assessment has shifted slowly but surely from the examination boards to the schools, and the workload has increased with the growth of criterion referencing.

Some of the anxiety and suspicion that seems to surround assessment, springs from our confusion about the range of purposes it serves, and about the difference between 'formative' and 'summative' procedures.

Formative and Summative

Formative assessment is an ongoing process, conducted both formally and informally, by which information and evidence about a child's learning is absorbed and used to plan the next step, or guide through a given task. In a class, a busy teacher may make an assessment decision every few minutes, and carry in his or her head a mass of information that will help to shape his or her professional activity. Without formative assessment teachers could not function effectively.

The mass of detail generated by formative assessment is useful for both teachers and learners, but less so for those not so centrally involved in the teaching process who need and deserve information periodically about the child. Parents are the main client group here, but there are many others such as other teachers and schools, providers of further education and training, potential employers, educational welfare officers, education psychologists and so on. For these groups, a summary is needed to provide an accurate picture of the child's learning and progress, without the burden of too much detail. Summarizing often feels very unsatisfactory. It flattens out the unique representation of the child as an individual, and sometimes

...the notion of labelling by level...

produces an image more crude and blurred than we would like, or even a caricature of reality. Adding grades or scores to this summative assessment almost adds insult to injury. The more child-centred we are, the more troubled we may be by the notion of 'labelling by level' that the National Curriculum framework could generate. Some summarizing, in communicating assessment, is probably inevitable. The challenge is to find a method that illuminates rather than removes the uniqueness of the child, and provides 'feedforward' as well as 'feedback', so that all the recipients of the information can take effective decisions about future action.

Approaches to Assessment

Norm-referenced Assessment

The judgements we make about children's learning may fall into three categories, depending on what we can take as the yardstick. If we are comparing the child with other children, or that mythical creature 'the average child', we are judging against a 'norm' or *norm-referencing*. This has been the traditional form of assessment for decades, in the British culture at least, and has therefore formed part or most of our educational experience, and that of the parents of our pupils. As soon as we establish 'norms' we classify according to 'pass' and 'fail', as a child's performance lies above or below the norm. We may also design our assessment in such a way that we spread the results in a neat 'normal' (bell-shaped) curve on either side of the norm, and be pleased that the assessment has properly stretched out the children to make comparisons between them easier.

Norm-referenced assessment is designed to enable comparative judgements, child against child, children again the norm. It is not designed to generate specific information about what an individual child knows, understands and can do, irrespective of other children. To fulfil this function, a completely different form of assessment is required — *criterion-referenced* assessment.

Criterion-referenced Assessment

To generate specific information about learning strengths and needs, the first step is to be clear about what is to be learned, and to describe those expectations as precisely as possible. The assessment procedure is then designed to provide evidence, for each child, of whether those specific expectations, or criteria for success, have been met. If the teacher's criteria have been designed to be within the extended grasp of the learners, and if teaching and learning have been effective, there is no reason why any of the children should 'fail'. Bell-shaped curves of results are irrelevant here.

Criterion-referenced assessment measures the child's performance against predetermined expectations, which are usually written down and built into the assessment process. If the expectations are expressed in vague forms, it is difficult to decide what constitutes successful achievement. If the criteria are highly specific, each one may be easier to judge, but there may be far more of them. The dilemma is compounded if teachers try to use the assessment criteria as their main learning targets. The more specific the criteria, the more arid, convergent and tedious may be our teaching. This dilemma lies at the heart of the National Curriculum framework.

To make matters even more complicated, national criteria for assessment, as enshrined in the attainment targets described in the ten levels of the National Curriculum framework, are all norm-based, that is they derive from the expectations of the people who wrote them about what a child *of a particular age* should know, understand or be able to do. There are major implications here for children who lie outside, above and below, the expected norms for their age group. They are entitled to inclusion in the national assessment process, but that very process will then describe them in terms of levels based on the norms for an age group.

Some areas of learning lend themselves more easily to criterion referencing than others. The more 'holistic' the learning, that is the more interdependent the different parts of learning, the more difficult it is to break down into specific, discrete, items. Even if you do manage to break it down, what actually makes for success in learning here is not just progress with the fragmented bits, but how the learner manages to fit them all together. In the 'Young Musician of the Year' competition, the judges are regularly asked what they are looking for in making their judgement. One judge might emphasize

*Attainment targets...derive from expectations about what a child of a
particular age should know...*

one aspect of instrumental expertise, another sees something different, but at the end they all agree that one of the most important criteria is 'musicality'. They may not be able to articulate what
'musicality' is, but they recognise it when they hear it. Teachers of
art and English, and others too, will sometimes find specific criterion
referencing too fragmented or too mechanistic to be comfortable for
them.

In all areas of learning, people's minds actually work in different
ways, and this may have a bearing on the specialism each of us may
gravitate towards. It may also be one reason why, in a secondary
school, certain subject specialists sometimes find little in common
with each other. I am reminded of a Secondary Headteacher's story
about asking her Heads of Departments to write down their teaching
objectives for the first year in the school — what we now call Year
Seven. The Head of Chemistry (what does that tell you about the
way science was organized?) produced several sides itemizing precisely what children were expected to do and learn. From the Head

of English she received a small piece of paper, and written on it the words, 'Our aim is to unlock the treasure house of literature'. I would love to be a fly on the wall when these two talk about assessment.

Differing approaches to curriculum may also underpin another of the difficulties that criterion referencing appears to present. The process requires us to write down what we expect to be assessable outcomes of our teaching. If our aim is to present children with a stimulus and promote in the children a spontaneous, creative response, it defies this aim to attempt to predict specifically what it is we expect them to do. Creativity and criterion referencing do not sit easily together. In the creative process, the only criteria that matter fundamentally are those that spring from the people involved. Their intentions can become the criteria by which they, or others, could assess what they achieve. A national framework of criteria cannot cope with such considerations, and this fact alone causes unease among many teachers.

Ipsative-referenced Assessment

This is the assessment process by which a child's performance is measured against that same child's previous performance. We use it to gauge individual progress over time. The word 'ipsative' derives from the Latin word for self — 'ipse'. Ipsative assessment can be highly specific (i.e. examining learning in a particular area or skill) or it can be more general. In either case, any norm-based or norm-referenced judgement is misplaced. We are interested only in this particular child, regardless of any expectations we may have of any other children. Such a process is comfortably child-centred, and acceptable even to those who find any comparative judgement objectionable. It is vitally important for parents too, who, more than anyone else, understand the unique complexity of their own children, and the dangers of judging them too simplistically in relation to others. If we wish, we can use the National Curriculum levels framework as a means of charting an individual child's progress over time, regarding level numbers merely as 'markers' and ignoring their normative basis. But the ten-level structure may be too crude to be really helpful here. Only a small proportion of pupils would expect to reach level 9 or 10 by the age of 16 years. The average child might aspire at that age to about level 6, after 11 years of compulsory schooling. His or her progress through the levels will be quite slow on this basis, perhaps staying at the same level for 2 years in some cases. The calibration is not really fine enough to meet the need for meaningful ipsative information, from one year to the next.

Criteria for Effective Assessment

The trends in assessment over the past several years have been clear and apparently inexorable. Norm referencing has given way to criterion referencing in all but a few areas of external assessment, with Advanced Level examinations being among the slowest to move. The range and specificity of the criteria have increased, to include assessment of the process of learning as well as the product. Assessment is expected to be more diagnostic and formative in purpose, to have a greater impact on our planning of children's learning, and on progression from one learning environment to the next, within schools and between schools. Information resulting from assessment procedures is both more specific, and more subject to public and parental scrutiny. Teachers bear greater responsibility for the judgements that are made. This may be in recognition of the professionalism of the teacher, or a means of limiting the cost of the process but, either way, teachers are now more accountable for their decisions.

Now, more than ever before, we need to be clear about what constitutes effective school-based assessment. There are four main areas to be considered: three are concerned with the technicalities of assessment, and the fourth with keeping it all manageable without distorting the balance in our teaching between presenting the input and observing the output. As Adrian Mole was to discover, measuring something does not necessarily make it grow!

Fitness for Purpose

Sounds obvious, doesn't it! There are several quite distinct reasons why we assess learning, and it helps enormously, on each occasion, to know why we are doing this — whatever it is — and who it is for. Similarly, we have at our disposal a considerable range of assessment techniques. Who should assess? It could be the teacher herself, or the pupil, or other teachers, or other pupils, or any combination of these. How should the assessment be done? It could be a formal procedure with desks in rows, no books, no talking, limited time, written questions and written responses. It could be by observation of children as they work normally in the classroom, laboratory, workshop or gym. It could be by listening to a child tell the answers to questions he or she has been asked, or by looking at what a pupil has produced. There are as many styles of assessment as there are styles of teaching and learning. The 'fitness for purpose' principle requires us to be clear about why we are assessing, and then to find the most appropriate techniques or styles to fulfil that purpose. Assessment, therefore, is a creative process that can be as varied and interesting as teaching and learning — it can be fun.

Clearly, there is a close connection between the way we plan teaching and the way we plan assessment. But which comes first? To quote the Task Group on Assessment and Testing (TGAT) report, yet again: 'The assessment process itself should not determine what is to be taught and learned'. This is easy to say, and vital to remember. However, it is not always easy to act upon, particularly when we are anxious about our accountability for the 'results' our children produce, and when the assessment criteria — statements of attainment, at levels — are 'writ large' in statutory orders. The greater your professional confidence, the more likely you are to put teaching and learning needs first, and let assessment adopt its appropriate place, as the servant of the curriculum. In National Curriculum terms, start your planning from the Programmes of Study, not the attainment targets.

Validity

This is an essential criterion for good assessment. In fact, if an assessment is 'invalid' it probably is not worth doing at all. But what does 'validity' mean? It is one of those esoteric terms that sounds as though it ought to be immediately intelligible. However, the more books on assessment you read, the more confused you can become, so let me attempt a common-sense definition in the hope that the technical experts will not find this too simplistic.

The basic idea is to ensure that your assessment tells you what you planned to find out. I sat in a fairly high-powered meeting once, and heard an academic colleague mention the WYTIWYG principle. Nods all round. I kept quiet — like you do — and wondered 'what is he talking about?' Finally I asked. WYTIWYG stands for 'What You

Test Is What You Get'. This is part of the validity idea: your 'test' or assessment has to focus on what you want to find out about. The questions you ask should be central to what you have asked the pupils to learn, not peripheral or 'trick' questions.

Nevertheless, 'content validity' is not enough. The way in which assessment tasks are presented to pupils, and what they are expected to do within them also has an important bearing on the result. We might call it the HYTIWYG principle: 'How You Test Is What You Get'. The aim of your assessment should be to allow each child the best opportunity to show you what you are actually looking for. An invalid assessment is one where the context, or structure, or requirements of the assessment task actually get in the way, and may prevent a pupil from showing you the reality of what he or she knows and can do.

All sorts of things can be at issue here. A child who is a poor reader may not be able to read the question he or she is given and does not therefore know what you want, which he or she might have been able to manage if the question had been posed a different way. That same child might have difficulty with a multi-choice test where each alternative answer could contain words that he or she does not recognize. The child who writes well, but very slowly, could be inhibited by a writing task to be completed in a time period just too short to allow him or her to finish. In each of these cases, what we have actually been assessing is not the understanding that we start out to check, but other things such as reading and speed writing.

Clearly, it is possible for the same assessment to be valid for one child and less valid, even invalid, for another because children have different ways of receiving and presenting information. Some read well, others do not. Some children can explain orally far more successfully than they can in writing, while others would express themselves by diagrams or drawings, using a minimum of words.

The practical implications of the pursuit of validity in assessment are as crucial as the theoretical. Absolute validity is impossible in reality: working teachers in real classrooms with real children have neither the time, the resources, nor the mind-reading abilities it would take to be certain that our assessment tasks can tap the reality of what is inside the children's heads. We can only do the best we can: manageability is the main constraint, and I return to this a little further on, after some consideration of the next piece in the conceptual jigsaw — that of reliability.

Teachers…have neither the time, the resources nor the mind-reading abilities it would take to…tap the reality of what is inside the children's heads. We can only do the best we can…

Reliability

Assessment is a human process that is subject to all the variables such a process entails. The pursuit of reliability involves recognizing the possible variables that could affect the outcome of assessment, and reducing them as far as we can. For the purposes of Teacher Assessment, there are four major variables to be considered:

1. Interpretation of the given criteria for assessment;
2. Levels of teacher involvement and intervention in the conduct of the assessment task;
3. 'Rater' variables — the perception of the person making the assessment, that is the teacher; and
4. The circumstances and environment in which assessment takes place.

The theoretical books on assessment will cover more detail than this, involving some heavy statistical analysis, but these will suffice for a start, if we explore them one at a time.

Interpretation of the Given Criteria for Assessment

It is quite clear that criterion-referenced assessment is now the model and for the foreseeable future. We have already seen that in order to be useful for assessment purposes, criteria have to be written with care, to be specific as possible. Absolute incontrovertible accuracy with words is extremely difficult to achieve. Those who framed the statements of attainment within the National Curriculum faced this challenge, and however precise they have tried to be, their words are still subject to interpretation by those who need to apply them. Difficulties abound. What is the difference between 'know' and 'understand'? What does 'reading fluently' actually mean? What constitutes a 'simple' explanation? Teachers can, and do, argue among themselves about these, and many others, and the discussion may help to clarify. Differing interpretations of criteria constitute a major variable in the assessment process, which we must try to overcome, to be fair to our pupils.

Take a particular example, from the National Curriculum science attainment targets. One of the statements of attainment reads, 'Pupils should know that living things respond to seasonal and daily changes'. In neighbouring classrooms in the same school, two teachers are working with two comparable groups of children. Each of the teachers thinks that he or she knows what this statement means, and implies. In the first classroom, the teacher overhears a group of children talking about hibernation. One child explains clearly that her hedgehog goes to sleep in a box during the winter, and she has learned from you that bears do the same — but not in a box. You reach for your checklist. More than one 'living thing' has been mentioned. Fine. Hibernation covers seasonal changes. That should do it. Tick in the box. Now you've only got the other thirty-one children to find out about.

Meanwhile, next door, your colleague has also been talking about hibernation. In a similar group, she too has overheard a child giving two examples of animals that hibernate, but she does not reach for the checklist, not yet. Only two living things were mentioned after all, just once, and there's still that bit about 'daily changes'. A week later, the same child, given a prompt to say a little more, talks at great length about seasonal activity, and about the way his baby sister behaves at different times of the day. Getting closer. A few more days pass, and the teacher gives all the children a quick matching exercise, designed to check whether they have remembered what they have heard and discussed about seasonal and daily changes and how living things respond to them. When the child completes the exercise to the teacher's satisfaction, then, and only then, will she accept that this criterion has been achieved, and she's still not sure whether the child would remember as much in 2 months time as he does now.

Both these teachers have acted quite properly in their own terms; what they have not done is agreed between themselves what they would accept as evidence that the criterion has been achieved. The ticks in their respective record books — if this is the way they have agreed to record their observations — look identical but they mean very different things.

The only way to begin to overcome this problem is to talk to each other, not about every individual statement of attainment, but first about your general expectations. Will you accept a child's chance remark as evidence of knowledge, or would you want to re-check with the child later? What's an acceptable delay between teaching something and assessing it, if you want to assess formally? Have you discussed what the child 'has done', and 'can do'? No assessment process, by the way, can ever be used to predict with absolute accuracy what a child will still know or be able to do at some point in the future. The best we can do is to make an informed professional judgement at a point in time.

The best we can do is to make an informed, professional judgement at a point in time

Teacher Intervention

Developments in approaches to assessment have highlighted the role of the teacher as a possible variable, which was not so critical in more traditional assessment processes. In the good/bad old days, at least so far as external assessment was concerned, the teacher's role was limited mainly to 'invigilation'. Schools organizing external examinations had to keep examination papers secure, make sure desks were a certain distance apart, issue numbers and instructions to candidates and ensure that the examination was conducted according to the rules. We were operating as supervisors not as teachers.

Changes in the examination system and the development of Standard Assessment Tasks and Teacher Assessment have brought the assessment process closer to the experience of teaching and learning. The teacher's role in the process is central and active. During Standard Assessment Tasks (SATs) teachers will have quite clear guidelines about how to conduct the tasks that are provided, but they will still function as teachers, promoting and guiding children where necessary. It would be quite impossible merely to 'invigilate' a SAT that might involve the children for several hours, spread over several days.

If teachers are actively involved with children during this process, at what point does that involvement affect the result to an 'unacceptable' degree? What's the difference between prompting, helping, showing them what to do, and doing it for them? Only discussion can really clarify this, but take one example we have looked at before, about the response of living things to seasonal changes. We have heard the child talking about hedgehogs going to sleep in winter and we want to check a little further. We could ask a 'closed' question that requires just a 'yes/no' answer. 'Do bears go to sleep in winter as well?', but here the question itself pushes the child firmly in a particular direction. Instead, we could ask a more 'open' question, 'Do any other animals do the same?' If the answer is 'Yes', then, 'Tell me about some of them'. We all know from experience that different types of questioning can produce quite different responses, and leave more or less room for the child's own decision or judgement to show through. All this now has a crucial bearing on the reliability of our assessment decisions, and needs to be shared with colleagues making the same assessments, so that all our pupils can have a fair chance to be judged on the same basis.

Other 'Rater' Variables

Differing styles of teacher intervention is certainly one type of 'rater' variable, the 'rater' being the person making the assessment. More subtle than that, but often as important in their impact, are the preconceptions we sometimes have already in our heads about particular children or groups of children, which can, almost unawares, have an impact on what we perceive as we make decisions about the children and their attainment.

All sorts of considerations can affect our expectations of children, and our perceptions of what they actually do. Some of us, for example, may still have different expectations of girls than boys, purely because of gender difference. If a child is from a particular ethnic background, we may assume that he or she would be skilled in something, or find something else hard, because we categorize this child as a member of a group, and generalize about the group, including the child.

Sometimes these distinctions are very subtle. We may respond to children's accents, and the clothes they wear; even the first name may indicate something about the child's socio-economic background, and from it we make other assumptions about motivation or aspirations or parental involvement. Sometimes the appearance of a child's name on a list can spark connections with other children who share the same family name and may be related, and we find ourselves making assumptions about the child before he or she has even arrived in school. These assumptions, when they occur, may raise or lower our expectations of the child's attainment. 'Selective perception' can then gather the evidence that may reinforce these expectations. It is a complex and difficult cycle that is sometimes quite hard to deal with: the first important step is to recognize that these assumptions do occur, that as human beings we are all capable of making them, and sometimes they can adversely affect the reliability of our judgement.

The 'halo' effect, and its reverse the 'horns' effect, are both well-known phenomena in assessment. We make an accurate judgement of attainment, and then extrapolate from that into other areas, assuming that if the child can do this, then it automatically follows that he can do that. If the child reads well then he should write well. If the child writes badly, she probably also thinks illogically, and so on. The appearance of a child's work can often be a major distracter from recognizing its other qualities, or lack of them.

The Circumstances of Assessment

The clearest example of this factor at work, we can probably find within our own experience of assessment. Take your mind back to the external examination experience that we all went through at school or college. Picture that large space, full of carefully spaced desks, books out of reach, with no talking. Remember the way the question paper was placed faced down in front of you and you could turn it over only when told to do so. Even the memory of those rituals is enough to make your pulse race a little or provoke feelings of anxiety or excitement. Circumstances affect performance, without doubt, and children react to the circumstances of formal assessment in different and sometimes unpredictable ways. The pursuit of reliability, therefore, also tells us, as assessors, to consider the circumstances we create as the background to the assessments we make, and to reduce this potential variable so far as we can. Try to keep the circumstances close to what the children are used to. Some circumstantial variables can be foreseen: BCG tests can wreck a lesson as the children troop in and out and inspect each others' arms, and they can certainly render unreliable any assessment you might be attempting at the time. If the fire-alarm goes off in the middle of the test or crucial group discussion, you could carry on, but be aware that the 'results' may not be worth taking note of. Friday afternoon, when both you and the children may be tired, is certainly not a good time to make a reliable judgement of a child's learning.

Manageability

I have made reference already to the 'jargon' of assessment, because it forms part of the way assessment ideas are often categorized, and to that degree is useful. Sometimes the technical terms seem to cloud the issue rather than clarify. Most of what we can say under headings of 'validity' or 'reliability' is just professional good sense by another name. All I am trying to do here is make intelligible some ideas about assessment that could improve the quality of what we do while keeping sight of what is actually realistic. There is nothing arcane or technical about the issue of manageability, which is close to the thinking of every teacher and school. In real situations in school, your aim of high-quality assessment procedures will inevitably be constrained by the resources at your disposal, of which the most crucial is your own time and energy. What you are aiming for is a 'best-fit' model (Fig. 1).

The needs of validity often seem to be opposed to the manageability of a particular assessment procedure. The most easily managed assessment could be a quick, simple, multi-choice test administered to lots of children simultaneously in a large and easily supervised space, with each child using a sharp HB pencil so that their papers can be checked with an optical mark reader attached to a computer to crunch the numbers, and a word-processor and printer to churn out the results. For some purposes, at some times, and for some areas of learning, this process might work, but it will certainly fail the 'fitness for purpose' and 'validity' checks on other occasions.

Trying to get as close as we can to the reality of what a child knows or understands may involve techniques far more subtle and individualized than a multi-choice test. Talking with a child is more likely to produce evidence of real understanding than any amount of writing or ticks in boxes, but talking to an individual child is hard to manage for any length of time in a busy classroom. If it is important to have that uninterrupted conversation, you may have to plan ahead quite specifically to allow it to happen, a theme I return to in the next chapter.

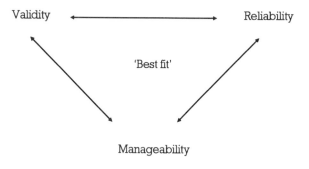

Figure 1 A 'best fit' model for high-quality assessment

Standardizing and Moderation

If our assessments are to be reliable, we try to reduce the variables that may affect the judgements we make. These variables often involve the human element — our understanding of the meaning of words, or our perception and expectations of particular children. To tackle them, we will need to share some of our thinking about learning tasks, criteria and children to smooth out the differences between us before we make a judgement. This process, which will take place within schools and between schools before Teacher Assessment is complete, is called 'standardization'.

Standardization

The very name gives a clue to the nature of the exercise: we are trying to find a consensus about 'standards', which is not always easy. In some schools, especially those that have been unaffected by GCSE requirements, teachers have traditionally worked quite separately from their colleagues. Teaching plans are drawn up in isolation from each other, learning tasks and assessment are conducted 'privately': expectations and standards may be discussed but not very specifically, and where colleagues disagree it is not considered significant. The process of standardization challenges the extent of teacher autonomy, by asking teachers not only to share their standards, but also to find a consensus that everyone is prepared to accept in determining what constitutes achievement of a particular criterion at a given level. The discussion is not merely an intellectual one. Teachers' standards are often held dear, as an integral part of our professional self-image. We are affectively involved, therefore, and feelings can run high. What begins as a discussion about a child's work and what it signifies can slip into a personal argument, in which we lose the distinction between what we *do* and what we *are*. Standardization is greatly helped by a prevailing atmosphere of professional confidence, mutual respect and a wish to find consensus, in the best interests of the children.

You may like to take some time to consider what the potential benefits of effective standardization can be, and what difficulties the process could encounter. If you feel it is something to be done only to meet statutory requirements it may feel like an added inconvenient extra: if you can find benefit in the process for both yourselves and your pupils you may approach it more positively.

One of the differences between standardization and moderation is that one takes place before the assessment judgement is made, and the other afterwards. The National Curriculum Assessment arrangements for Key Stage One give responsibility for this process to the local education authorities. LEAs appoint part-time 'moderators' whose first task is to work with a cluster of schools assisting in the 'standardizing' process, both within each school and among them. The moderators, working as a team, help to encourage shared standards across the LEA. They will visit schools during the conduct of the Standard Assessment Tasks (SATs), and afterwards may help schools to decide what to do if there is a discrepancy between the child's profile component level as determined by Teacher Assessment and the profile component adjusted to incorporate the attainment target level determined by the SAT. In one important respect this post-assessment adjustment, rather inaccurately called 'moderation', is unlike the 'moderation' conducted after some GCSE examinations. If the SAT produces an AT level that is different from your teacher assessment, the SAT level is 'preferred' to yours, but only in that particular target. The rest of your Teacher Assessment judgements are not affected: they will not all be scaled up or down as a result, as they might be in the GCSE moderating process.

So far, we have looked in fairly general terms at the basic principals of assessment: referencing, fitness for purposes, validity, reliability and standardization. One significant part of the framework of ideas has not been mentioned so far, that of differentiation — the means by which we establish what the differences between children's learning are. The purpose may be to establish the particular next steps the child needs, or to report to parents and others what level of attainment has been reached to date. Differentiation raises some issues of principle, and important practical implications, which open the following chapter.

Chapter Two:
Managing Assessment

In this chapter, we shall look at the practical implications of managing assessment and suggest some strategies that might make the current expectations more achievable. Manageability, of course, is an imponderable, depending on all sorts of considerations including our mood, confidence and energy level. It also presents busy teachers with a dilemma: the assessment techniques that are the easiest to manage may be the least effective in producing valid and reliable 'results'.

The first step in coping with this dilemma is to think carefully about your topic plans or schemes of work, to plan assessment into teaching rather than add it on as an afterthought. Differentiation is so central to this process, in terms of both learning and assessment, that it needs some explanation. If you are already familiar and comfortable with the notion of differentiation, skip this bit and join in later on.

Differentiation

This is another of those terms we come across frequently in the theoretical framework of teaching and assessment and is best explained in thoroughly practical terms. It starts from the assumption that learners learn at different rates, to different levels of attainment, and in different ways. All children are not the same but all of them, regardless of their differences, deserve to be offered equal opportunity to learn and develop; therefore they need equal access to the learning experiences we offer, and to recognition of their particular strengths and difficulties.

The arguments about how and why these differences exist are well-rehearsed. Some people say that the potential to learn is part of the genetic make-up we inherit from our parents. Others argue that social and environmental factors from the child's birth onwards have the greatest bearing on the child's capacity to learn. This 'nature/nurture' debate has occupied psychologists and educators for decades. If you believe that genetics is the sole determining factor in learning, teaching is reduced almost to child-minding, as nothing we do can really have an impact on the child. More common in some teaching is the view that socio-economic factors entirely beyond the control of the school are so strong that the teacher's role in really developing children is really quite limited. If we believe this, our expectations of children may be reduced as a result. This is a basic teaching dilemma, in mainstream and special education. None of us want to push children so hard towards attainment beyond their reach that they face continual failure. If we make them stretch too far they may fall flat again and again. Conversely, if we limit our expectations, we may not challenge and extend the children at all. The art of teaching is the use of professional expertise, experience and intuition to offer children learning challenges that are within their *extended* grasp requiring effort to reach, and occasional failure too, but never so dispiriting that the child's self-esteem is damaged and with it the motivation to keep trying.

So what has all this to do with differentiation? Differentiation in our teaching plans is about offering all the children we teach opportunities within their extended grasp, so that each of them has equal opportunity to make progress. Differentiation in assessment is about constructing assessment tasks that allow each child the chance to demonstrate what he or she can do, to help us to see the differences between their attainments and needs.

There are two approaches to differentiation, which can apply to both learning and assessment. Differentiation by outcome offers all the children in a group the same learning experience or assessment task, and the differences between the children are recognized in the outcomes of the task. There are some real problems here for assessment that need to be explored further. One of the purposes of assessment is to distinguish individual children's attainment to date and needs for the future. The task you create for them may be too complex in wording or structure to allow lower-attaining or less-confident children the chance to show you what they have learned. The task feels and sounds too hard for them and they freeze up, or panic, or guess wildly. Some years ago, administering a standardized test that was the same for all the children in a year group, I watched a child sit quietly crying onto her test paper, which was just too much for her. For that child, that test gave her no opportunity to show what she could do.

For children at the other end of the range in terms of attainment and personal confidence, differentiation by outcome can fail in its purpose because the children take a quick look at the problem, work out the answer quickly in their heads and present it, without bothering to show the step by step process by which they arrive at it. In other cases, the very quick-thinking children may not use the opportunity to show the full extent of what they can do, contenting themselves with just answering the question as it stands and then moving on.

Differentiation by outcome can fail in its purpose...

There have been, and still are, heated arguments among assessment 'experts' about the difficulties and benefits of differentiation by outcome. What everyone would agree on, however, is that making differentiation by outcome effective is very difficult, requiring very careful construction of the task to overcome possible disadvantages to learners at either end of the attainment range.

Differentiation by task is the other major approach that can be adopted in assessment, and in teaching. It means offering children learning or assessment experiences that are specifically designed to cater for their particular levels of attainment. By carefully matching the level of task to the level of the child, we can avoid some of the difficulties involved with differentiation by outcome. We can make sure that the language level and structure of the task guide the child into the activities that give us the information we need to make our assessment. The brighter child will be stimulated to show the full extent of his or her capabilities. The less-bright child will not be outfaced by the sheer complexity of the task. The assessment will, hopefully, confirm the judgement we made in the beginning about which task to offer to which child.

But what if that initial judgement we made in allocating the child to the task was not really accurate, or was affected by some stereotypical expectations of the group with which we identify this child? Either the child is obviously misplaced and we have to change the task, or the child may rise or fall to the expectations we have exemplified in our choice to task. How do we then know what they might be really capable of if we had offered a different challenge? Obviously, the extreme form of differentiation by task is as potentially unhelpful as the extreme form of differentiation by outcome. To avoid prejudging the issue too much, we need to widen the opportunity, and make the boundaries of the task a little wider to allow children to move beyond the range of expectations we had for them. Decisions about differentiation are central to the structure of Standard Assessment Tasks as well as to school-based teacher assessment.

Obviously differentiation issues affect the way we organize learning as well as assessment. Setting and streaming are a form of differentiation by task — mixed-ability teaching reflects differentiation by outcome. All the considerations are equally relevant and reinforce what we already know about good mixed-ability teaching requiring learning tasks differentiated into, perhaps, three levels to allow all children appropriate equal access. A further issue in planning both learning and assessment is taking account of the different preferred learning styles of different children, and this will be built into our planning agenda.

Planning Assessment into Teaching

Formative assessment is part of the upward spiral of teaching and learning. This spiral operates at the level of individual children and their teachers, and at the level of the whole school. There is nothing new about that. The diagrammatic representation of the assessment cycle in Figure 2 is very familiar, but I have added the National Curriculum terminology to bring it up to date.

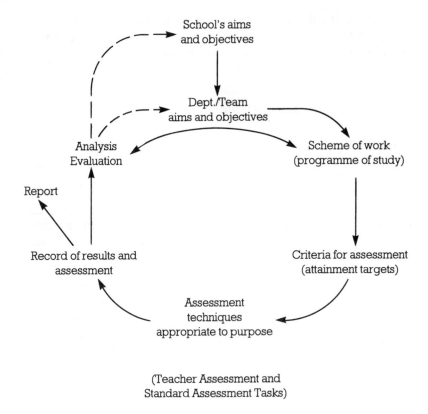

Figure 2 The assessment cycle

Please note: All the features of this cycle are interconnected and should be internally coherent

If assessment is accepted as a central feature of the education process, then it follows that it deserves a central place in our thinking and planning of teaching, at a whole-school level as well as at the level of teacher teams and individuals. It follows too that it cannot be divorced from delivery of a required, or centrally determined curriculum: in National Curriculum terms, therefore, it has to start with the Programmes of Study, which are described — but not necessarily delivered — in '*subject-specific*' statutory orders for each 'subject' area in the National Curriculum framework. Chapter Five in this book looks at the whole-school management issues. What I want to cover here are the stages that teachers individually, or in teams might go through to ensure that assessment is purposeful, valid, reliable and manageable in the real situation.

Start with the Programmes of Study

The statutory requirement states that children are entitled to have the programme of study described in each curriculum area offered to them during the key stage. There are four key stages, each related to a chronological phase in the child's development. Key Stage One covers the years from the fifth birthday to the end of the school year in which the child reaches his or her seventh birthday, (Year Two). Key Stage Two covers Years Three to Six, aged 7-plus years to 11-plus. Key Stage Three covers Years Seven to Nine, and Key Stage Four covers Years Ten and Eleven. These stages are unequal in length: Key Stage One for some children will be only five terms in length, while Key Stage Two will be twelve terms. The key stages also, in some systems, cut across the institutional framework, with children transferring from one school to the next in the middle of a Key Stage. This has great implications for curriculum planning in systems with middle schools, which might cover the latter years of Key Stage Two, and the early years of Key Stage Three. The ten levels of attainment described by TGAT are only loosely connected to chronological age, and attempt to describe age-related norms, which could be expected of the 'average' child at a particular age. We already know that the spread of children's attainment at a particular age is very wide: at age 14 years, for example, we can expect children to be operating at any of the ten levels. More of the implications of this are described later.

The first step in curriculum planning, therefore, is to check your existing plans, topics, schemes of work against the programme(s) of study for the key stage, look for the mismatch if it occurs and amend your plans accordingly if necessary. Planning for just 1 year at a time will not be enough here: the person who teaches children in the final year of the key stage does not want to be left picking up the pieces of the programme(s) of study that have not been covered so far, regardless of whether they make sense to the pupils and constitute a coherent and stimulating progression from previous learning. Planning over the key stage is essential to make the process work educationally — a real challenge to 'middle-school' systems, or to any school where each teacher has been left alone to decide what he or she may tackle in any one school year. Planning curriculum together, as a team, is a very helpful first step towards standardizing, as the discussion will be about our expectations of learners, and interpretation of the programmes of study.

From Learning Objectives to Assessment Objectives

Once the overall curriculum plan has been determined, this can be broken down into chunks, or topics, projects, modules, units, or any other term we care to use. This may cause some trouble theoretically for those teachers who regard their curriculum as a 'seamless robe' and dislike dividing it up in any way at all. In reality, practically all teachers do just that, trying to ensure of course that the 'chunks' relate to each other and do not fragment the learning experiences of the children.

For each chunk, let's call it a topic, the learning objectives should be clear, and will affect not only the content to be offered, but also the ways in which we decide how children should work. If one of the learning objectives, for example, is that children work together through a problem-solving exercise, then they need to work in groups rather than on their own, and the layout of the room will reflect that need. Many teachers, having clarified their objectives, involve the children themselves in discussing and deciding *how* those objectives could be met, given the constraints of space, resources and time available. The clearer the objectives, the more possible and fruitful it is to share with pupils, so that they know what to expect, and what may be expected of them.

Another useful step at this stage is to ask yourself whether the learning activities you are planning, and the ways you will present them, provide access for all the pupils they are intended for. Are they differentiated, for the ability levels, learning pace and preferred learning styles of all the children in the group? All of us, as learners, are more effective with one style or another — through listening, or talking with others, or writing, or drawing, or with practical activities or cerebral ones. The main essential is to provide a range of teaching styles, to correspond to this range of learning styles, to avoid over-reliance on one style, which could be boring and put some children at a disadvantage by not providing learning opportunities that are the most fruitful for them.

The topic plan and its learning objectives will, in turn, provide assessment opportunities, which can be used if necessary or desirable, to determine what children are attaining and to provide evidence of progress to date. Let me share a problematic scenario I came across in some schools in the early days of National Curriculum implementation. Teachers had identified learning objectives, and thereby assessment opportunities, and then proceeded to try to use all those opportunities, to assess formally everything that was being learned by every child. This turned into the 'roller-skates and clip-board' routine as boxes (usually relating to individual statements of attainment) were ticked and mounds of data generated, which the exhausted teacher was not too sure what to do with. The *quantity* of assessment was too great, the quality was almost inevitably poor, and the cry that assessment interrupts teaching rose to a crescendo.

To avoid this thoroughly unnecessary and frustrating situation, another planning stage is essential, to decide which of the assessment opportunities we actually want, or need, to make use of. Several factors may have a bearing on this decision. If anxiety about National Curriculum accountability is a major factor, then it helps to consider the statements of attainment in terms of the *frequency* with which they are encountered as children progress through the key stage. By the end of the key stage, all the attainment targets will have been checked, but some of them are encountered regularly, while others may only crop up once or twice.

The 'frequent' statements or targets certainly do not need to be monitored, assessed and recorded each time they occur. They may form part of our annual report to parents, and therefore need to be looked at systematically for each child over the course of a school year, but not each time they occur. One of the English attainment targets, for example (AT1, Speaking and Listening) occurs almost continually, not only in English but all over the curriculum, and we can choose which assessment opportunities provide us with evidence on which to make an informed judgement. Other individual statements of attainment derive from learning activities that may take place quite rarely. When these occur, the teacher will need to have planned to make an assessment, realizing that this particular activity may not occur again for quite some time, if at all, during the key stage. This analysis of the 'frequency' of individual targets or statements is one of the factors in planning assessment objectives for any one topic. It enables the teacher, for example, to phase her observa-

This particular activity may not occur again for quite some time, if at all...

tion of children over a longer period of time, and stretch her assessment activities thin, to keep them as manageable as possible.

Another factor when determining assessment objectives may be the particular focus of a topic. Some topics lend themselves to evidence of particular knowledge, understanding or skill. That does not mean, of course, that all other aspects of learning are ignored by the teacher or the children, but one facet of the children's learning becomes prominent for that particular time. This too allows the children, who are told what the particular focus may be, to show what they can do and see how that fits in to the overall monitoring of their capabilities. Where the teacher knows her pupils well, she may be able to identify and pursue different assessment objectives for different children in the group working through the same topic, as she builds up her evidence across the range of criteria and the range of children. This capacity to individualize assessment obviously is a function of the number of children a teacher will encounter in any one week or timetable cycle. As a history teacher in a secondary school, I might see over one hundred and fifty children in any one week, and that alone would affect my capacity to know all those children as individuals, however talented and energetic a teacher I might be.

Planning for Assessment Objectives

By now, by a planning method that suits your particular circum-stances, capacities, and the range of criteria you are dealing with, you should have some assessment objectives for the topic under consideration. These will be always fewer in number than the full set of assessment opportunities that the topic could provide. Having reduced the quantity of the assessment load, however, we need to be careful about the quality. 'Assess less better' seems to be the motto here. As part of the topic plan, it might be helpful to list your assessment objectives as part of a grid format, and then add the decisions you need to make in each case. It is worth planning quite specifically to address these questions. For each assessment objec-tive, who will do the assessment and by what methods? What record-keeping will be needed? How will you manage the class-room to enable this assessment to take place? What evidence of the children's attainment will/could this topic or activity provide?

In Chapter Three, I deal in detail with issues of record-keeping and evidence, but we need to explore here the question of choice of assessment strategy and classroom management.

Choosing the Assessment Strategy

The art of assessment, as we saw in Chapter One, is to find the best fit between purpose, validity, reliability and manageability. Easy to say, but much harder to do — particularly as these considerations sometimes seem to pull us in different directions. At its simplest, the choice is between several techniques we have at our disposal. We can assess by asking children to write down, or draw, or present to us graphically, or speak the answers to tasks or questions we can present to them in writing, or orally, or in visual or graphic terms. If the assessment objective is a practical one, to check whether chil-dren can perform a given task, then we need to observe what they do. That 'doing' may, in turn, be affected by how we present the task to them in the first place. If the purpose of our assessment is to place children in a rank order, we need to be clear about what that rank order is based on. It could be the speed by which the child completes the task, or the arriving at a correct answer, or it could be the 'elegance' of the procedure the child goes through, in reaching the correct answer in a mathematical problem, for example. If, on the other hand, we are assessing to decide whether a child has achieved a particular 'criterion' (*i.e.* a prespecified objective, or statement of attainment) we are not concerned with measuring the child against other children, but only with measuring the child's performance against the requirements of the criterion. In other words, we need first to know why, for what purpose, we are doing the assessment before we decide the particular approach we need to use.

Next, the nature of the child's activity will determine what we actually do to make the assessment. If the child has to speak, we need to listen; if the child has to perform a particular task, we need to watch, with as much focus and attention as we can manage; if the child needs to write or draw, we need to read or look at their efforts. Where there is a tangible product, we might choose to look at this away from the children, in the staff room, or at home. If there is no tangible product, the assessment has to be done at the time, in the classroom, which raises all the issues about classroom and time management.

A further set of considerations comes from our pursuit of validity: that is, our attempt to give children the best possible opportunity to show us what they can do, and know, and understand. Many children are able to explain their knowledge or understanding of something more effectively by speech rather than in writing. Setting children a 'knowledge' test, which requires them to read a question and then write a response, may be relatively easy to manage, but it may give a false impression. We may have placed an unnecessary barrier, for some children, between their knowledge and their means of expressing and communicating that knowledge. What we end up finding out, for these children, is not actually what they know about volcanoes or Ohm's law, but how good they are at reading and writing, or sitting quietly, or working to a time deadline. If we want to use the written stimulus or question as part of the assessment, we need to be careful about the language level and complexity of the structures we use, to make sure that we are not unfairly disadvantaging some children. To take this one stage further: if we believe that children learn in different ways and we therefore offer a variety of ways of learning in the activities we plan for them, we should also be prepared to offer as wide a range of *assessment* styles as we can. Apart from anything else, it gets assessment away from the traditional straight-jacket of the 'test', makes it more varied and more fun, and lets children experience assessment as a part of teaching and learning, rather than something different, or an after-thought, divorced from the context and circumstances that have generated their learning.

Finally, and crucially, comes the question of classroom management. As we have seen earlier, careful forward planning can make it easier, by reducing the sheer quantity of assessment activities that need to be undertaken. The question to be answered in this planning is 'How much assessment is needed?', not 'How much assessment is possible?'. Other strategies will help also in reducing the workload still further. One of them stems from the realization of how broad National Curriculum levels actually are. Remember there are ten levels specified, spread over 11 years of compulsory schooling. Level Ten will be accessible to only a small proportion of children before the age of 16 years: we can expect most children to cover perhaps six or seven levels during their compulsory education, which means that their progressions through those levels will be quite slow, perhaps taking 2 years in some cases to move through one level to the next. There are implications in this for the expectations of parents, which I shall turn to later. In planning assessment, it helps to realize that frequent detailed checks on children's levels will be neither necessary nor desirable, as they move slowly through the framework. Once we are familiar with the targets and statements, and have discussed them with colleagues as part of the standardizing process, the decision about many children will become easier, as they are seen generally to fall well within the boundaries of a particular level. This may be more difficult if there are multiple statements of attainment to take account of.

As a first step therefore, try to observe each child in the group or class for a little while, and find how many of them you can quite easily place at one level or another. Inevitably, there will be some children you are unsure about, whose 'performance' seems erratic or very patchy, or you feel the need to look at more closely, for all sorts of reasons. These may well be children who seem to be at the level boundaries, or for whom it is just too early to tell where they are. No one who understands the complexity and subtlety of this process will expect you to produce instantaneous and simultaneous assessments of all the children you encounter. Making your decisions in some cases will take quite a long time. One final suggestion about this 'impression' level definition (which may be your starting point): 'impression' decisions have to be done quite carefully, as they can be affected by some variables that could render them unreliable. One of these is the personal impression we may have of the children: as we explored in Chapter One, all of us are capable of making assumptions about children based on some stereotyped judgements that we carry around with us. Secondly, and just as subtle, is our tendency to replace specific criteria for judgement by a comparison between one child and another. If you reckon one child is operating at level five, and you are not sure about another child but have the idea that she is 'better' than the first one, you might be tempted on those grounds to go for level six, instead of realizing how broad level five is, and that it can encompass children who are obviously not 'the same'.

Classroom management techniques become paramount as soon as we start to focus attention on individual children, rather than 'scanning' the classroom to ensure that, generally, learning is taking place. Your own teaching style is a critical factor: if you are 'instructing' children and the central focus of the lesson is you, you cannot easily focus on an individual or group, leaving the rest to their own devices. You need to incorporate into your teaching style some methods that encourage and enable pupils to be less dependent on you, to release you, for probably only a few minutes at a time, to observe, listen, make a few 'field notes' of what you see and hear.

Even with young children, it is possible to provide a learning environment that encourages them to be more self-sufficient. The children need to know, for example, where various items of equipment are and how to use them safely without coming to you. Learning materials need to be self-explanatory and accessible. Encouraging collaborative group work skills helps, and other approaches that allow teachers to circulate, talk to individuals, mark work alongside children rather than away from them, work closely with this group today, that group tomorrow, and so on. Obviously, children can work effectively this way for only part of the time. They need the stimulus of good direct instruction and explanation, and the cohering 'presence' of the teacher to motivate and challenge them, but it is possible to plan the variety of teaching and learning styles to meet both the children's needs and yours, without the 'guilt' that you may feel if the children are self-reliant to the point where they do not seem to need you like they used to. 'Letting go' is part of helping children to become autonomous learners, like we do as parents to help our children grow into adulthood. The whole idea worries some teachers as they expect the classroom to descend into chaos as they lose control, but taking the process one step at a time may produce not only more time for assessment and observation but also more effective learning for the children and a greater sense of responsibility for themselves, which can improve the overall atmosphere of the classroom and the school.

To sum up, there is a very close connection between delivery of National Curriculum Assessment, teaching and learning styles, and classroom management. This understanding may help teachers who are not yet involved in full National Curriculum implementation and are looking for an effective way of preparing themselves. They would be best advised to do a preliminary 'audit' or review of their current curriculum, so that this is ready to be matched against the statutory Programmes of Study when they come 'on stream'. A review of assessment methods and record-keeping could then follow, to gear up for the criterion-referenced assessment that the National Curriculum entails. The implications for teaching and learning styles should then emerge, with methods needed to enable the teacher to observe individual children systematically, by arranging the classroom and the available learning resources in such a way that children are able to work occasionally without direct intervention from the teacher. Beyond that, the main needs are not to panic, and to keeping thinking and talking to each other: the more team work, the better.

Finally, one small example of how some of the teachers I have been working with have tackled the issue of time to assess children as they work. A group of Year Two teachers were discussing their strategies. One of them explained that she had talked to her children about her need to take time to observe and listen to them. She told them simply why she needed to do this, and they discussed what this might involve, for her and for them. One of the children reminded her of a story they had read together in which one of the characters had a cloak that made him invisible. 'That's what you need, Miss'. So an agreement was reached. The teacher would bring in a cloak, and promise to wear it in class for only a few minutes at a time, during which she was 'invisible' and the children would interrupt her only in an emergency, leaving her free to watch and listen to them, and make her notes. They went further, and arranged what to do when the children got stuck, or needed help from her during the few minutes each day she might be wearing her

The children would interrupt her only in an emergency

cloak. There would be 'stuck book' in one corner of the classroom where a child could write his or her name, and a range of activities available there to keep the child occupied until the teacher was able to take the cloak off, 'return' to them and check the book to see who needed help. Other teachers in the same group from different schools offered similar strategies they had worked out: one wore a special hat when she was 'assessing', another put a little notice on her table. Small simple strategies and, as ever with children, subject to the unexpected things that happen in classrooms, but nevertheless helpful. In particular, the children themselves understood what was happening and why, and had taken one step towards the realization that teaching and learning are a partnership, with assessment an essential part of it.

If children of 6 years of age can understand these ideas put to them at the right level, then children at all ages in school can do the same. As our experience of recording achievement in the secondary sector has shown us, children and young people are capable of helping themselves and their teachers in the continual process of planning and monitoring their own learning and development, if we encourage them to do so.

Finding and Managing Time

There is little doubt that finding and managing time is one of the major anxieties all teachers have. When I am working with teachers, primary and secondary, about the implications of current developments, 'time to do it' figures high in their lists of concerns. There are no easy and absolute answers: all I offer here are some suggestions about how to tackle that task, based on experience, some of which you may find helpful in your own particular circumstances.

Time for What?

Break the issue down by asking yourself, 'time for what?'. Different aspects of the assessment tasks require different kinds of time. Sometimes it will be time with children in the classroom. Other time will be needed to think and plan on your own, and different time again to think and plan collectively with your colleagues, in a small team or across the whole school. As you start to plan you need 'development time': when you get going in the classroom you need 'maintenance time'. Development time will be a high priority to begin with, but the need for it will decrease as you establish workable plans: maintenance time will always be needed, to make your observations and keep your records updated, but that time may also decrease over a period as you become more familiar with the criteria, streamline the procedures and gain confidence.

Do Not Skimp Development Time

Try not to avoid or skimp development time in the rush to 'get started'. Inadequate planning will probably increase the 'maintenance time' requirement and still leave you feeling dissatisfied. You may be very busy but still unsure that you are achieving very much.

Plan Assessment Priorities

Plan your topics and schemes of work and make the necessary choices about assessment priorities. By planning over a year, and broad-brush planning over the key stage, you will be able to stretch the assessment workload more thinly, without the lurking anxiety that unforeseen 'chickens' will come home to roost as the end of the key stage approaches.

Review Assessment Routines

Review all your present assessment routines, 'marking', internal tests and examinations, ongoing assessment of reading or practical skills, to satisfy yourself that all your current assessment time is really well spent and time-effective. Try to change these routines to meet current needs, not just add to them.

Incorporate National Curriculum into Normal Routine

Incorporate assessment for National Curriculum purposes in to your normal routines, by connecting your regular assessment criteria to the framework of statutory criteria, at least in part.

Review Current Assessment and Record-keeping Procedures

As a team, department or whole school, review all your current assessment and record-keeping procedures. Check what procedures you will need to have in place, and consider the gap between *status quo* and these new needs. Plan to bridge the gap by establishing short-, medium- and long-term steps to be taken. These clear plans, once established, can serve as a reassurance to parents, governors, and the LEA who are interested in the school's development. The identified steps and time scale can help you to evaluate your own progress and raise your confidence that the step-by-step approach is working.

Involve the Children

Involve the children themselves so far as their age and stage will allow to consider how classroom time and tasks can be managed. If they are able to help by taking some responsibility for this, all the better.

Observe Available Non- contact Time

In primary schools, where non-contact time is not so widely available for every teacher as in the secondary school, take a collective look at the non-contact time available across the school, and how it is currently used. In the early development period of managing assessment, you may want to deploy any existing non-contact time differently. It may be possible, occasionally, to allow two teachers to meet to discuss their plans, or to do some informal standardizing, or make some observations of children together. Or it may even be possible to give each teacher 1 hour a week to allow him or her to observe children without interruption, or to update his or her records in peace.

Consider Team Teaching

Consider the possibilities of occasional team teaching, if class size and available space allows for it. It takes planning but can be great fun, and allows one teacher to 'manage' the classroom while the other can make closer observation of individual children, or work with them more directly.

Get Second Opinions

As a means of getting a 'second opinion' about a child whose assessment is proving problematic, arrange to swap classes for half a day with a colleague. You ask her to focus on the child or children about whom you are unsure, and she will do the same for you in your class. Another teacher's slightly more distanced view of the child can sometimes save you time in coming to a conclusion.

Involve Other Adults

In primary schools particularly, but possibly in secondary schools too, look at the possibilities of involving adults other than the teachers in the classroom process. It is neither reasonable nor reliable to ask another adult to make an assessment, but he or she could manage some aspect of classroom activity, allowing you to focus more quickly on the particular assessment activity you want to undertake.

Do Not Assess Too Much

Try not to let anxiety about 'accountability' push you into assessing too much. During the first year of GCSE assessment, when some teachers were more centrally involved than they had been before, more assessment was done, in some cases, than was necessary. Quantity of assessment is no real substitute for quality, and quality assessment takes time to plan and to do.

Do Not Panic

Above all, do not panic. At the end of the day your judgement about level, or any other assessment you make about the child, is an informed and professionally derived best guess. Setting yourself achievable targets, reaching them and moving on will probably produce better results than herculean efforts to do everything all at once, which may leave you too exhausted to teach effectively. One of the educational entitlements that does *not* appear in the legislation is the entitlement of the child to daily contact with a teacher or teachers who are healthy, sane, optimistic and confident. Clear collective goals, one step at a time, will be more productive all round than trying to do too much too quickly.

Chapter Three: Keeping Records and Evidence

Record-keeping

As with the consideration of assessment procedures, the first questions to be asked when thinking about record-keeping are 'Why are we doing this? Who is it for?'. These are straightforward questions that raise some fairly straightforward answers. Clearly, a prime purpose of record-keeping is to help us monitor the progress of individual learners and to plan for each child's next learning steps — in other words, a formative purpose. Secondly, these formative records will need to be summarized periodically to provide information for others, parents mainly, who are entitled to and deserve information about their children that is based on a systematic monitoring process. Thirdly, and particularly relevant in the current climate, we keep records to show that we have undertaken statutory responsibilities, such as delivering the National Curriculum and monitoring children's progress through the framework of targets and levels. This latter purpose is thus mainly about accountability, which figures so largely in the Education Act of 1988, and about which the teaching profession may have mixed feelings. Of course, accountability is not new, but it now has a legal/contractual edge to it that was not so apparent before when accountability for record-keeping might have taken the form of periodic submission of one's record book to the headteacher, to ensure that work was being set and marked. One interesting item in the National Curriculum regulations states that parents can have access to their child's Attainment Target record at any time, given 15 days' notice to the school — just one symptom of the changing nature of accountability.

There are three main reasons for keeping records, therefore: to monitor and plan ahead, to inform others, and to demonstrate that these purposes are being properly pursued. None of these are new, but criterion referencing generates a greater quantity of specific information to be recorded, and adds considerably to the potential workload involved. On the subject of workload, it is always worth remembering just how much time we currently spend on gathering and recording the growing amounts of information about children at school. To do this, make a quick list of all the records and reports you and your school already make. These will range from records of standardized reading tests, through daily 'marking' records and internal examinations, to confidential references, data for 'statement-ing' procedures or the careers service, application forms for higher education entry, and so on. The list will be quite long: for each item, ask yourselves some simple questions like 'Why do we do this? Who is it for? Does what we do really match up with the original purpose? What happens to the data we collect and record? Who actually uses it, if anyone, and for what? Do any of these systems overlap? Could they be organized more rationally, to save time and effort? Would information-technology application help? How much time does all this take us? Is it time well-spent?' Some schools discover in this exercise that considerable time and effort could be saved, and that they could change their approaches to record-keeping to meet new requirements without adding too much to their workload.

What are these new requirements? And what systems of record-keeping are appropriate to an assessment process that is largely criterion-referenced? Some school records will continue to be kept in much the same ways as before. The attendance register, for example, is a vital record and has to be treated carefully as befits a legal document. The 'pastoral' record too will give necessary details for each child of address, date of birth, emergency contact numbers, and so on. Computerization is already having an impact on such records, and will continue to do so. Beyond these, what records do all teachers need to have? The scheme of work or curriculum plan is a record of teaching intent. Schools now are clarifying the connection between these plans and the National Curriculum Programmes of Study, as a check for themselves, and to demonstrate to the governing body, for example, that the school is planning to fulfil its statutory obligation to its parental community. This curriculum plan can then form the basis of a *post-hoc* record of teaching undertaken. This record, if it details the learning activities, and gives some indication of when these took place, can be a way of showing the next teacher, the next school, or the interested parent the context in which particular learning took place. Say, for example, you were discussing with a parent the child's attainment target record and interest was shown in what had led you to indicate a particular level of attainment. An important part of your response could be the curriculum record, which shows you what the children were actually doing at the time you were gathering your evidence. This adds context to a record from which such a context is missing. Statements of attainment and attainment targets, as with most other 'performance criteria' are 'de-contextualized', and all our experience of recording achievement has shown us that de-contextualized statements are not very illuminating or meaningful for parents or others not centrally involved in the learning process. This experience should have implications for how we report to parents, of which more is said in the next chapter. The curriculum plan, connected by some form of annotation to the National Curriculum framework, and possibly dated too as children work through it, can be an important part of our record-keeping. It is a record of curriculum coverage.

How might we need to change our record or mark books to meet the needs of a criterion-referenced assessment process? To work this out, let us identify an end-point need and work backwards. The statutory record-keeping need is now clear. By the end of the Key Stage, teachers are expected to have made and recorded a judgement about each child's level of attainment for each attainment target. There will be expectations to this general requirement, where for very particular reasons a child may have been exempted from some part of the National Curriculum framework. These reasons may be connected with the 'statementing' procedures for children with special needs, in mainstream schools or special education. There may be other particular circumstances, which lead to temporary exemption, such as long-term illness or absence from school. For these and other 'special needs' considerations you might wish to look at 'Curriculum Guidance Two: A Curriculum For All', published by the National Curriculum Council.

The attainment target record is central to National Curriculum implementation, available to parents who wish to see it, transferred with the child from one school to the next, and part of the information on which the child's statutory level of attainment will be determined at the end of each key stage. What records will the teacher need and want to keep to enable her to complete this AT record professionally and to her own satisfaction?

Most teachers already keep a 'mark book' of some kind, in which they record marks, grades, scores or comments pertaining to work produced by the children. My mark book, as a secondary history teacher, had a big double page for each class I taught, with children's names listed down the left hand side, and then lots of little boxes. At the top of each column I would write, in very small and abbreviated writing, the title and date of work set, or a grade, or whatever annotation I chose to use. This record would provide a quick visual check on the completion of work, or absence, and a rough impression of progress being made, or not as the case may be. It took me hours to mark and record the work, but in today's circumstances I would need to do something quite different.

For a start, my mark book would need to reflect a connection with the framework of targets, statements and levels in my 'subject' and possibly in other 'subjects' too. My history teaching, for example, would provide plenty of evidence of children speaking and listening, reading and writing, all of which are English attainment targets. Leaving such cross-curricular implications aside for a moment, my mark book would need to reflect the assessment objectives I had decided upon in my assessment planning. Given that I and my colleagues planned our assessment objectives in such a way to provide evidence of all the attainment targets over the key stage, the judgements made about these assessment objectives would feed into the attainment target record, which I would update periodically as my more-detailed records accumulated week by week, term by term.

This 'mark book' might only cover work that produced a tangible product, such as a piece of writing, drawing, map or diagram, which could be graded and annotated. Many of the attainment criteria we are looking for in children's work do not involve a tangible product that can be taken away and looked at without the children present. Incidentally, marking work alongside the child is very effective for giving meaningful feedback, but I know how hard that may be to manage. If assessment is going on actually in the classroom, by observation or by listening, a different type of record may be needed, which I have referred to elsewhere as 'field notes'. Primary school teachers often tell me that they should not need to keep notes because they have always managed to keep their observations of children in their heads. The problem now is that the number of items they may need to check, given the number and range of the statements of attainment, is just too great to allow our memories to handle and store them, and then we tend to remember selectively with all the problems that may entail. As already seen, growing familiarity with the criteria over the years will help us to make quite fast decisions about some children but others will require a more specific and structured focus, and it is in these circumstances that 'field notes' may be needed.

Field notes are really the quickest, simplest form you can find of jotting down key things that you see and hear, which can be used later to remind yourself what happened without relying entirely on your memory. I have come across two sorts of field notes, one in which the main focus is a specific criterion or statement of attainment, and another in which the main focus is an individual child. Take the criterion-based type first. Let us say that you want to check out a particular task or area of learning for a child or small group of children for whom you have not been able to reach a conclusion by means of your general daily observation. You set up the task, and arrange the activities of the other children in such a way that they are gainfully occupied in relevant learning but do not need direct attention for a few minutes, leaving you free(ish) to focus on the individual or small group. You will have decided beforehand what you are looking for, in these particular children. You may already have drawn up a basic structured record to make the job easier for you, with the names of the children and the things you are looking for, so that all you have to do as you watch and listen is make a few marks, any symbols that are meaningful to you, but do not need to be meaningful to anyone else. Field notes are personal, idiosyncratic, and as simple as you choose to make them, in fact the simpler the better.

I often work with teachers writing their own guidelines for assessment by observation, which includes the development of manageable field notes. Almost every time the same dilemma emerges to be discussed. Surely, someone will say, we cannot always predict what a child will do and say in response to a particular task. Can we therefore prestructure our field notes at all, or will that very structure limit what we may see or hear? Yes of course it could, but putting no structure into your record can be hard to manage, and may take too much of the precious time you have managed to put aside for your observation. A compromise might then be discussed, with a structured part of your observation together with an unstructured part, to note these unexpected but significant things that may happen as the children work on the task. Teachers' preferences about the amount of structure in an observation field-notes record vary: you need to find the method you feel most comfortable with, and amend however and whenever you feel the need. You may decide, too, that you do not need to keep field notes after you have used them to help you

make a decision about a particular child. I can think of some circumstances, however, in which you might want to keep them, as extra
evidence to support a judgement that you guess might be contentious or queried in the future. I have often asked myself whether
teachers will be tempted to keep more evidence for those children
whose parents are teachers, and who may therefore know the right
questions to ask about their child's learning.

Parents are teachers...

The second form of field notes is different in one major respect to
the first, in that it takes as its first principle the overall learning and
development of individual children. It may be, therefore, that this
method is more manageable the fewer children you are actually
responsible for. Keeping notes on individuals when you have one
class or group is a different task than when you may see up to two
hundred children in a week, or even more, as is the case for some
secondary school specialists.

The framework for this method is much looser. For each class you
teach, you would need an exercise book, with sufficient pages to
allow one or even a double page for each child, whose name would
go at the top of the page. You keep this book close at hand when
you are with the group. As you watch and listen and work with child-

ren you will be aware occasionally that something in an individual child's response or behaviour strikes you as interesting or significant. The child may, for example, begin to use vocabulary that indicates he or she has grasped an idea, or to approach a problem in a more advanced way than before. Your observation may be triggered by your familiarity with the external National Curriculum framework of statements and levels, but may also be a part of a much wider perception of learning and development, unrelated to the relatively narrow, 'subject' base of the National Curriculum. Whenever you have the opportunity, at the time or shortly afterwards, you find the page in your book related to the child in question and make the briefest note you can of what you have seen and heard, and date it. Inevitably, some children draw your attention more frequently than others. From time to time, perhaps as the time for updating the child's attainment target (AT) record approaches, or before you next see the parents, you flick through your book and notice that there are several items noted for one child and nothing at all for another. That should be a prompt to plan to focus on a 'missing' child when you get the opportunity: for the period of a full day, or a single session you could remind yourself to speak to and watch that child more clearly whenever you get the chance and try to record what you notice. This too may prompt you, if you can manage it, to offer the child activities that might help you to fill the gaps in your perception of the child. Many primary teachers tell me they already keep a log or diary that is based on individual children: the benefit of adding the kind of structure I have described is that it gives you a fast visual check to help make your observation of children a little more systematic.

In the secondary school such individualized systems are more rare, because of the numbers of children involved. Some teachers already have such a system and, if something like this becomes a habit, it can save much time later — when reports have to be written, or information offered to special needs procedures, the next teacher or school, or child's tutor. Here, as elsewhere in this business, manageability is the key to effective systems, but manageability is a vague concept, like the length of a piece of string. What one teacher would consider unmanageable another will do as a matter of course, so great are the variables involved.

One way to make record-keeping more manageable without jeopardizing your own professionalism is to identify areas in which pupils can take a productive part in keeping their own records, having been taught how, and subject to the 'quality control' checks the teacher might need to do.

Involving Pupils in Record- keeping

In all learning programmes, and in some parts of the National Curriculum framework, there are some activities and experiences that need monitoring but do not involve professional judgement as to the quality of the outcome. In English, for example, we need to keep track of the range of writing modes children have tackled, the variety of books and materials they have read, the different contexts for oral work they have experienced. As we share expectations and criteria with the children, we can arrange for each of them to keep a record of these kinds of activities for themselves, at the back of an exercise book or file, or in a separate pre-structured record we could design for this purpose. Children could begin to be involved in the maintenance of such a descriptive (as opposed to evaluative) record as soon as they are old enough to understand what is involved and skilled enough to write down or fill in the required format.

The process of Recording Achievement, which has been piloted, evaluated and written about extensively, offers us many examples, from children of all ages and abilities, of methods of involving children in keeping track of their own progress and development. Helping children to be so involved has demonstrable positive results in motivating them and thereby producing greater effort and commitment, and that alone has encouraged many schools and teachers to share assessment and record-keeping with children. From the purely logistical standpoint, too, greater pupil involvement can be helpful, as the demands of record-keeping grow in step with the specificity and quantity of areas to be monitored. Whether the motive for involving children is child-centred or logistical, the first essential step is to discuss quite overtly with children, in terms that are appropriate to their age and stage, the principles of assessment and record-keeping we are now dealing with. These principles are not inherently difficult, and once grasped by the children can, through them, be shared with their parents more effectively than by means of formal written communication alone. Many schools and teachers are already sharing the National Curriculum with their pupils, and even translating the attainment targets and statements into child-friendly versions, to help the children to understand and keep track of their own learning more effectively. Pupils' assistance with record-keeping, where it is appropriate, can be enormously fruitful, and worth the thinking and development time that it may take to establish.

Evidence

The notion of evidence has cropped up repeatedly in both this chapter and the previous one, and usually figures prominently in school-based discussion about assessment within and beyond the National Curriculum framework. This may be a good time to examine it in more detail.

To begin with, we need to accept that very little in assessment can ever be proved beyond reasonable doubt. Assessing children's learning is an art, not a science; it is a human process exercised by human beings with other human beings and therefore subject to so

Very little in assessment can be proved beyond reasonable doubt

many unquantifiable variables that we can only try to get as close as we can to reality, accepting that both judgement and supportive evidence can never be described as incontrovertible. That said, it helps to define the nature of the evidence we might be gathering as part of an assessment process. Some quick definitions may help: some evidence may be tangible and *retainable*, such as a piece of writing, a map, a diagram, a model or a chart. Other evidence might be *ephemeral*, such as a question or an action — it happens and we see and hear it but the moment passes and the evidence is gone. Another distinction can be made between '*primary*' evidence, produced by learners themselves, and '*secondary*' evidence, produced by someone else but based on what the learner did. These terms are as an historian might use them.

To test out these distinctions, and their implications, try and relate them to your own teaching experience. Think about a topic or activity you presented recently to your pupils. What were your teaching intentions or objectives? What did the pupils actually do during this activity? By the end of it, what evidence was there of what the pupils had learned? Think broadly about the evidence, including the ephemeral, what was said, or even a child's expression, as well as the more obviously tangible things like a test score, or a poem, or whatever else the activity might have generated. If you go through the items of evidence that occur to you that were based on that activity, see if you can categorize them into ephemeral and retainable. You will see how crucial the ephemeral evidence often is as the basis for the decisions we make about pupils' learning to date and relevant next steps. Anything on your list that has involved you making a judgement or a record (*i.e.* marks, scores, observation checklists or comments) is the secondary evidence base, and some of that will be a way of making primary ephemeral evidence retainable. In addition, you may find other means of capturing the ephemeral, by using tape, camera or video; this is a direct way of doing the job but has still relied to some degree on the judgement of the person controlling the equipment, choosing the photograph or editing the tape.

We actually generate more evidence of children's learning in the course of our normal teaching than we would want or need to keep. Discussions of evidence often focus on storage, how many filing cabinets or even prefab. huts you would need in which to keep everything, and visions of children leaving school with wheelbarrows full of files, photos, models and so on. Obviously we have to be selective, and make decisions about what evidence to keep and what to let go. Sometimes we use the camera to turn three-dimensional evidence into two-dimensional, or use a record as a substitute for unwieldy primary evidence. Essentially, we have to decide, yet again, why we are doing this and who for, before we can develop any reasonable criteria for what to keep, where, in what form, for how long and so on.

What are the possible reasons for keeping evidence? You could ask yourself this, based on the same activity and its evidence you considered a few minutes ago. For what reasons would you want to keep any of this? Who might find it useful?

There are several purposes that we could pursue. We might keep something that shows a particular strength or talent a child has, or a particular difficulty. We might use the example of learning difficulty as the 'before' part of a 'before-and-after' sequence, showing how progress has been made over a period of time. To do this you would need to date both items, and annotate them briefly to show why they have been selected. There might be something that the child's parent or even future employer or further education provider might be interested in, or the next teacher or school. A different purpose again would be served by finding and retaining some evidence that seems to you to exemplify a particular statement or level, to check with other colleagues that they feel the same, as a part of the standardizing process. If you know that a particular child's performance is inconsistent from one part of his learning to another, and this might be of concern to the next teacher or parent, you might keep something that illustrates the difficulty and indicates specifically where and how improvements could be made. Also there is much to be gained from involving the children themselves in considering and selecting items from their own learning that they enjoy or are proud of, or would like to keep for whatever reason. Choices by very young children might be very personal to them. As children grow, and as we share with them the criteria for success that we are seeking to demonstrate, the children can become active participants in the process of identifying their own evidence of attainment. Many teachers have involved pupils in this way at GCSE level, and such systems clearly have a place in any assessment process where the criteria are identified and can be shared with the learners.

All these notions, different forms of evidence, its significance for different purposes, the logistical considerations of access and storage, will need to be thought through and discussed to meet the particular circumstances of your school, yourselves and your pupils. There will be no statutory prescription of required evidence, but schools and LEAs will need to have some guidelines, to ensure some sensible coherence and to reassure teachers. It needs to be said clearly, for example, that teachers will not need to have primary evidence to support every assessment judgement, and the teachers' records, based on valid and reliable assessment activities, are an essential part of the evidence base. Evidence can be helpful and illuminating, for us, for children, parents and other teachers, and needs to be approached from that perspective, rather than some spurious pursuit of proof.

Portfolios

There is nothing at all new about the idea of a portfolio to house evidence of attainment for a variety of purposes. Art and design have always used such a process, and many primary as well as secondary school teachers have begun to keep folders or files containing carefully selected evidence to exemplify children's learning. The recording achievement process, as it has developed over the past few years, has the selection and presentation of evidence as one of its central features. And now the National Curriculum too involves an evidence base for our judgements, and as an aid to communicating and adding meaning and context to otherwise de-contextualized targets and levels. For the secondary school organized on subject-specific lines, this gathering of evidence may mean a portfolio for each child in each subject. Cost considerations will ensure that such folders are as cheap and simple as possible, and storage and access will also have to be thought through as the process develops.

Chapter Four:
Communicating Assessment

Both this chapter and the preceding one should be headed by a pithy and appropriate borrowing of a phrase beloved by computer buffs — 'Rubbish in, rubbish out'. In other words, the information we communicate to others can only be as useful and valid as the original assessment procedures that generated the information in the first place. In these days of glossy school brochures and marketing, we have to remind ourselves to put as much energy into getting the basics right as we do into 'presentation'.

Given, therefore, that we have tackled the basics to ensure that assessment information is as accurate, valid, standardized and purposeful as we can manage, we need to look at how this information is communicated to others. In many respects, the traditional methods of offering feedback on educational attainment are not terribly promising. All of us remember our old reports from school, with those ever-present grades, positions in class, and euphemistic comments about effort and progress. For those of us taking external examinations, the formal feedback provided on our efforts was subject to long delay, and coded by global numbers or grades, which were arrived at by mysterious means behind closed doors. Much has changed over the past decade in secondary schools: single-sheet reports with one line per subject have been largely replaced by the 'cheque book' style report, but A to E gradings still abound, perhaps expanded into words ranging from 'Excellent' to 'Cause for concern' but not much more meaningful. In primary schools, methods of reporting to parents have varied widely although some uniformity is now demanded by the National Curriculum arrangements.

The gradual trend towards criterion-referenced assessment, accelerated by the impact of National Curriculum, necessitates a review of how information about children's learning is presented. In this chapter, we need to look at meeting the information needs of the 'clients', the children themselves, their parents, the next teacher and school, and those to whom young people go at the age 16 or 18 years for the next stage in their education, training or employment. Here again, fitness for purpose is the criterion for effective communication and these various client groups do not necessarily have the same needs.

Communicating with Learners

Running as a thread throughout this book is the importance of sharing our objectives with learners, and involving them in planning how those objectives might best be met, judged and recorded. Once we have achieved the necessary clarity to communicate these objectives, then the cycle of reflection and target-setting can begin and continue throughout the child's learning life, at school and beyond.

Traditional methods of offering feedback to learners have largely involved grades, marks and scores arrived at by a variety of means and often made meaningful only by comparing one child's performance with another. If all we ever offer learners is a number or grade as feedback, no wonder they try to make sense of it by comparing their performance with each other. There have always been exceptions to this of course: particular teachers, subject areas and schools in growing numbers over the past few years have succeeded in offering much more specific feedback, harder to use for comparative purposes but much more helpful to the learner in knowing what to do in order to improve. As learning objectives are shared, the learners themselves can be increasingly involved in monitoring their own progress, and the feedback becomes more integral to the process of teaching and learning.

Most teachers spend many hours every week checking and annotating childrens' work, for which the ostensible purpose is the offering of feedback to learners. Sometimes perhaps this purpose gets confused with the business of proving that work has been set and checked. Specific meaningful feedback takes time — time to write comments, time to mark alongside the child, and time to offer individual and collective oral feedback as a piece of work is discussed. Teachers' time and energy are not limitless, and we need to get the balance right between feedback and preparation. Like many other teachers, I found I could not settle to forward planning until the books had been marked, by which time I was often too tired to think creatively.

To find a better balance between 'marking' and 'planning' time, and to offer more helpful feedback, many teachers choose to 'focus' their marking, checking a particular item in the work set rather than everything. This is the sharp end of the distinction I drew earlier between learning objectives and assessment objectives. The distinction is never absolute, but can help to make assessment and communicating feedback to learners more manageable. In order to be effective in its prime purpose of enhancing future learning, feedback to learners (of any age) needs to be as specific as we can manage, positive as well as constructively critical, and always encouraging identification of the next necessary steps. Oral feedback is as helpful as written, although it may be harder to manage as it has to be offered when the children are with us, requiring time-management skills of a high order. Oral feedback, like oral evidence of learning, is ephemeral, may be forgotten by the child, and may not satisfy the underlying purpose of some 'marking' — to show that the teacher's work has been done.

As children become more involved with understanding objectives, with reflection and target-setting, they can also be more involved in providing feedback for each other, and for themselves. Self- and peer-assessment need to be preceded by identifying and discussing the criteria and what constitutes quality in their own and each others' work. This done, the feedback that learners receive from each other, which is specific, constructive and based on evidence, can be as valuable as that which they receive from teachers, and the teacher can put more of her energies into checking the quality of this feedback rather than providing it all herself.

Communicating with Parents

Very few, if any, of us would deny the centrality of the parents' role as partners with schools and teachers in the learning and development of the child. Clearly, therefore, we communicate with our pupils' parents not because of some statutory requirement but because we want and need to do so as effectively as possible. To achieve this at a time of rapid educational change is particularly problematic, and we need to share the nature and implications of current change before we can share meaningful information about children's progress through school. Teachers are one professional group whose 'clients', in this case parents, have themselves experienced the service, when they were at school themselves. There is inevitably, however, a generational gap between the parents' experience of school and their children's experience. This means that our job is not only to inform about current education provision, but in doing so tackle parents' existing knowledge and assumptions that stem from their own experience. The processes of teaching and learning have developed over the past 20 years, as might be expected, to meet the developing knowledge base, the expectations of the employment and training community, and as part of a natural evolutionary pursuit of more effective learning and preparation for adult life. Approaches to assessment have changed too, quite markedly, away from norm-referenced towards criterion-referenced assessment, from primarily external to more school-based procedures, from 'terminal' (end-of-course) to continual, involving the process as well as the product of learning. Public examinations at age 16+ years and beyond have changed too, and have, in turn, had a marked effect on assessment in other parts of the education service. There are mixed views, expressed as loudly outside the education service as within it, about whether these changes are positive or damaging to the interests of the nation's children but, either way, the change itself is clear.

Schools are now obliged, more than ever before, to offer information to parents. Before they can do so effectively, however, the first task is to explain the changed context within which this information needs to be set. Central and local government may offer some limited help with this task, but the school itself will no doubt bear the brunt of providing the necessary background information, either individually or in collaborative groups or consortia where common tasks can be sensibly shared. Leaflets and newsletters explaining the new curriculum and assessment framework in intelligible terms are an obvious place to start, to reach as many homes as possible. Meetings in school do not always attract as many parents as we would hope for, but the issue of assessment is of central concern to parents as it is to teachers and as each cohort of children nears the end of a key stage parental interest will rise. How we manage such meetings is a challenge too: too erudite and jargon-laden and we may confuse, too simplistic and we may patronize. Just as with good teaching, experiential methods are often effective in providing real understanding. We could enlist the help of the children themselves in providing activities for parents that illustrate the concepts of criterion-referenced assessment, and the norm-based

*Meetings at school do not always attract as many parents
as we would hope for*

levels of the National Curriculum structure. Schools that have arranged such learning opportunities for their parents have found that an experiential approach raises quite acute and fundamental discussion about the purposes of education, as well as illustrating what an *affective* impact assessment can have on all of us, and the way we feel about ourselves and each other.

In communicating to parents about their children's learning and progress schools normally use written reports and/or individual parents' meetings. Most secondary schools use both written and oral means: some primary schools have hitherto relied on oral communication alone. As the annual written report becomes a statutory requirement, schools will be reviewing their arrangements, and hopefully trying to ensure that we meet the real needs of parents as cost-effectively as possible.

*Communicating to parents needs to be done as cost-effectively
as possible*

The report at the end of each key stage may have a particular
emphasis on the level achieved in each 'subject' area, arrived at by
the bringing together of the teachers' judgements and those resulting from the Standard Assessment Tasks. Most written reports, however, will not necessarily follow this pattern, as numbered levels
may be difficult to determine with any accuracy before the final year
of the key stage. The reasons why levels may not be a useful part of
parental information during these intervening years may need to be
carefully explained to parents. Even if levels are offered, they will
need to be qualified to explain how they have been derived. Numbers are deceptively simple: they seem to offer information but by

over-simplifying they can obfuscate rather than clarify. More import-
antly, perhaps, the offering of numbers alone can result in us, both
parents and teachers, describing the unique complexity of a child or
young person in terms of a number, a prospect that personally, as
both parent and educator, I find quite appalling.

Quantified information, therefore, has never been and still is not
sufficient to describe the learning and development of pupils as they
grow. Reports to parents reflect not merely the relatively narrow
learning objectives of the National Curriculum, but also the wider
educational objectives of the school. We offer feedback to parents
about affective as well as cognitive development, personal and
social as well as academic learning, activities beyond as well as
within the classroom. We cannot overload the system by trying to
share information that is unnecessarily detailed, de-contextualized
and therefore fairly meaningless. We may need to regard the written report and the face-to-face parents' meetings as complementary
rather than separate events.

The criteria for an effective parental report are clearly emerging:
it should be comprehensive in its view of the child, qualitative as
well as quantitative, clear, concise and meaningful. Quite a challenge. To meet this challenge, within the existing parameters of time,
energy and resources that schools have at their disposal, under-
standable efforts have been made to 'kill two birds with one stone',
by developing a formative, classroom-based, recording system that
can be offered in identical form to the parents. To illustrate the difficulties here, let me describe the developments in some of the secondary schools I have worked with. In one case, departments have
responded to new criterion-referenced schemes in their subjects by
producing highly detailed assessment and recording systems, and
have computerized these to manage the mass of data more effectively. The detail is understood by the teachers, and the children too,
all of whom have been directly involved. The departments, faced
with new reporting requirements, now hope to offer these same detailed computerized records to parents each term or so, as they are
produced in school, in place of the traditional summary report. The
reaction of many parents has been predictable. They may be im-
pressed by the sheer weight of detail, but does it really help them to
understand what is happening? Do they have sufficient background
information to plough through and find meaning in what they are offered? What about the cost of the exercise, repeated for more children as the process spreads through the school?

Another typical scenario, again inspired by the potential cost-effectiveness of providing formative information for summative purposes, involves schools developing records of achievement. Quite rightly, the development has begun with teaching and learning, and teachers develop interesting and varied methods of involving children in reviewing and target-setting in the classroom. These reviews take place at appropriate times and intervals, and will vary in method, format and timing from one teacher or department to another. This reviewing has a prime purpose to involve pupils in activities that will help them learn more effectively.

Simultaneously, the school searches for a means of reporting that is capable of handling more specific information, and considers using the formative format for summative/reporting purposes. So far so good — but the conventions of parental reporting run deep. Parents have always had, and therefore expect, reports issued at set times of the year, within a given format common to all subject areas. The school, or at least the decision-makers in the school, believe that these expectations must continue to be met. The *ad hoc* and varied arrangements that have developed in the departments are replaced by a common format, to be completed at particular times regardless of whether the timing fits the teaching and learning opportunities. For the children, the process may become boring and repetitive as the connection is broken between learning and reviewing. The teachers come to regard 'reviewing' as 'more forms to be filled', to which they may have no particular loyalty. In this case, the perceived needs of parents for information offered in particular ways overrule the worth and relevance of the formative process. It does not have to be this way: many schools have managed to find an acceptable compromise between formative and summative purposes, but it is not easy. We may have to explain the implications of current change very carefully to parents, as well as teachers and children, in order to find a system that meets the criteria for effective reporting.

The written report is one way of communicating with parents: the other is by means of the parents' evenings, interviews or conferences. Many schools have developed different ways of organizing these over the past few years, and the parent-/client-oriented climate induced by the 1988 Education Act encouraged such a review. One major difference between primary and secondary practice may concern the availability of examples of the children's work, which adds context and meaning to the information we offer and the questions parents ask. In the primary school, the children's work is often on display, or available to be looked at as you wait to see the teacher. In many secondary parents' meetings, teacher and parent talk across an empty table, while the children stay at home, or wait outside.

Where the school is gathering evidence of children's work in subject-based portfolios, these could become the basis of discussion with a parent. One step further, children may already be involved in identifying and reviewing evidence of their own progress in the classroom, and use that as the basis of their tutorial review, in which pupil and tutor collate and synthesize the evidence (both primary and secondary) of attainment and progress. This same synthesis would be of great value to the parents, representing a summary arrived at by a structured process involving teachers, child and tutor. In schools that have come so far, the parents' meeting can take on a new perspective, as the children themselves, helped by their tutors, take their parents through their portfolios and share the learning targets that they have already identified with their teachers. The partnership between parent, child and school is enacted to the benefit of each of them.

All these possibilities are available to schools, to make their own decisions within the very basic framework established by statutory regulations. The attendance of the child at parents' meetings might be rejected out of hand, or restricted to children above a certain age, but at least the potential benefits and difficulties will have been discussed. Developing new systems always takes time to think and plan, but the actual running of a changed system need not take any longer than we have previously devoted to reporting and meetings that have not always fulfilled their ostensible purpose. If parents' meetings involve contact with all subject teachers, for example, some teachers will attend parents' evenings for each year of the school, and see each parent for only a few minutes. The system could be changed, with the tutor the first-line contact for the parents in his or her group, thus restricting the number to be seen, and enabling longer to be spent with each, with interviews spread over a longer period of time, at the convenience of both the tutor and the parents. There are costs and benefits of all the possible organizational structures: schools, teachers, parents and governors will all have views on this that need to be heard.

Communicating for Progression

We tend to discuss progression in terms of continuity between one school and the next, but the issues raised are pertinent also as the child moves within the same school from one teacher to the next. How do we communicate effectively to ensure that previous learning and experience are recognized and taken account of in planning the next learning stage, or in finding the best training or the most appropriate job? If our assessment and record-keeping systems are working well, there will be no shortage of information to share, but there will be decisions to be made about how much is useful, in what forms, when and for whom.

Information to communicate is not the only prerequisite: there also needs to be willingness to liaise professionally with colleagues in our own schools or others, and a removal of those barriers that have traditionally inhibited progression. One of these, without doubt, is the realization that the more we know about the pupils' previous learning and experience, the more we may need to amend our teaching plans and resources to suit the starting point of the learners. The National Curriculum structure has the potential to enhance progression, by clarifying curriculum entitlement at each key stage, and by encouraging teachers to standardize their assessment approaches before information is offered about attainment levels.

The information that schools will be statutorily required to pass on at transfer will probably remain as minimal and unhelpful as that which we are *required* to share with parents. If communication for progression is to be really effective it must move beyond numbers in boxes on an attainment target record and allow the more rounded picture of the learner to emerge.

The record of curriculum coverage will obviously be of interest to the next teacher or school — particularly where transfer takes place at ages that do not correspond to the end of a key stage. As teachers' assessment improves with practice and collective familiarity with the criteria, the quality of information about attainment should also rise, but again the context is missing, and little may be known about the ways in which the pupil learns. At every stage of transfer, teacher to teacher or school to school, a few carefully selected, dated and annotated examples of the children's work can be more meaningful, particularly to a fellow professional, than masses of de-contextualized information. Secondary school teachers sometimes are not sure how to handle portfolios of evidence that are beginning to be offered by primary schools. Discussion with primary colleagues about the purpose and the logistics of the exercise can produce a system that illustrates what primary colleagues, and the children themselves, wish to show the next school, and allows the particular examples to reach the tutor and/or the subject teachers who most need to see and use it.

Strategies for effective progression are currently being discussed and reviewed right through the education service, and ideas abound for enhancing not just the documentation but also the professional contact between teachers, to overcome the layers of distrust that have sometimes accumulated between one stage of the service and the next. Working in all parts of the service as I do, I hear the same arguments about progression voiced in colleges about schools, in secondary schools about junior schools, junior schools about infant schools, infant schools about nursery schools, and *vice versa*. No doubt colleagues in higher education say the same things about all of us.

The key issues in effective progression are discussed in greater depth in Chapter Five, and illuminated by the case studies. As the young person moves through school towards the end of compulsory education, the issue of communicating assessment becomes more complicated as the target audiences for such communication broaden to include further and higher education, training providers and employers. Much has been said and written about meeting the needs of these audiences, most recently through the introduction of a national record of achievement and individual action plans for young people. Inevitably, central prescription of the content and format of such a record tends to emphasize product rather than process, and here again we must constantly remind ourselves that the documentation is only ever as worthwhile as the information that it contains, and the validity of the procedures that have generated the information. It is worth recalling too, that the young person remains at the heart of the whole system. As the Chief Executive of the Chamber of Commerce in one of our major cities said to me as we discussed Records of Achievement for school leavers, 'What employers are really looking for is the young person who has experienced the process of reviewing, target setting and planning his or her own future'. We can see, also, that the distinction between 'formative' and 'summative' information is being blurred, as individual action planning, including targets for future education, training and employment, carry through from school and are incorporated into the adult lives of the young people in whatever sphere of activity they are involved.

For the most part, all the issues relevant to the communicating of assessment at any stage of the young person's progress through school apply equally to this particular stage. Information offered needs to be based on sound procedures, to reflect the whole person so far as that is possible, to place norm-based levels against the unique background of each student's talents, experiences, needs and aspirations, to be meaningful to and manageable by the receivers of the information. In one respect, however, the emphasis has developed significantly. By the age of 16 or 18 years young people need to be capable of presenting the information about themselves to people of their own choosing, whenever they are given the chance to do so. To do this effectively, they themselves need training as well as encouragement, and can reap the benefit of all our efforts to involve them in the process of learning, reviewing and future planning during their years at school. Experience of the process of recording achievement, particularly over the past decade, has taught us that real benefits accrue when children have been involved in such procedures from an early age, not starting at the age of 14 or 15 years with the onset of Technical and Vocational Education Initiatives or Compact. The 1990s can and should see students taking their rightful place in communicating assessment and presenting evidence of their own achievement and needs as the full potential of the National Curriculum is realized in schools.

Chapter Five:
Whole-school Issues

One of the difficulties in attempting to describe and discuss assessment is that it defies our need to label phenomena and treat them discretely, as separate entities. The means whereby we identify what children have learned are inextricably interwoven with the way we teach. In turn, too, the way we teach is interwoven with the way the school is managed, its collective goals and aspirations, and the prevailing atmosphere or ethos that affects all aspects of teachers' and learners' activities.

This chapter aims to explore several major whole-school issues: reviewing current practice, the development and monitoring of an overall policy on assessment, the management of cross-curricular assessment, and progression. Inevitably, we shall stray into more general issues of management, leaving you, the reader, to take some of the questions raised and consider them within the very specific context of how your own school or college functions as an organization. How does change happen in your school? To use the short-hand but graphic terminology, is it 'top-down', or 'bottom-up'? Is policy about something (*i.e.* special needs, equal opportunity) written by a person, or by a working party, or does everyone do their own thing? Who contributed to the development of your school's statement of aims? If a large number of people did so, how was the process managed? Within what time scale? Who were these aims written for? Is the language and structure appropriate for this target group? You probably know how your own organization functions, and much can be learned, positive and negative, from past experience.

Of course, the management of an organization as complex as a school cannot be reduced to a simple dichotomy of top-down or bottom-up. The two extremes are both problematic: policy written entirely and solely from the top will probably exist in name only, as the people who have to make it work will neither necessarily understand or accept it. Bottom-up development sounds ideally demo-

'How does change happen in your school?'

cratic, and might work given a strong collective urge to succeed, and plenty of time. Somewhere between the two is the combination of direction and collective involvement that will be the most effective, but the variables are too numerous to produce any one prescriptive model.

What follows are some suggestions about places to start, implications to consider, and blind alleys to avoid, based on schools' experience, which you may find helpful in your whole-school development.

Reviewing Current Procedures

An obvious, and useful, place to start when considering the development of whole-school polices and procedures for assessment, recording and reporting is with a review of your own current practice. To be really effective some preconditions are worth mentioning. Firstly, it helps to offer everyone involved in such a review time and opportunity to read and talk through the basic conceptual framework of assessment. For some teachers this may be quite unnecessary, but a remarkable number of us have trained and worked as teachers without ever coming across a thorough explanation of assessment issues. It helps to know enough to use the terminology accurately, and to recognize the criteria by which to determine the validity, or appropriacy, or reliability, of the assessment we do as part of our normal teaching. Another necessary precondition of a review of current practice is some degree of confidence that, where the review illuminates areas we need or want to change, then that change could actually take place. In some of the schools I work with, staff resistance to review is high because they tell me they have been there before, with analyses complete, suggestions made, reports written, which then disappear from sight and never re-emerge. That may be because the ideas for change do not take account of the realities and the resource limitations that the senior managers know about but have not shared. It follows, surely, that all relevant information about resources that could affect the implementation of the policy to be developed needs to be aired and shared *before* the ideas are generated. To do otherwise is to set ourselves up for failure and frustration.

A third precondition for effective policy development across a school is to give individuals and teams the chance to review their own practice, as classroom teachers and as a section or department before asking them to share their thinking with others. When a consensus is being sought, some compromise is inevitable: real collaboration is more likely if individuals and teams are confident and generous with each other rather than unsure of themselves, and consequently defensive with others. My basic assumption here, which others might dispute, is that clarity leads to confidence, and confidence enhances collaboration.

A Structured Review of Current Practice in Assessment

If you want to start at the level of the individual there are some basic questions you could ask yourself, to clarify and analyse what you currently do. Check these out for yourself, as honestly as you can. In your own classroom (or laboratory, or workshop, or gymnasium, or whatever you teach):

- What do you assess?
- What methods do you use? Observation? Written tests? Talking and listening to pupils?

- Why do you do what you do? To give feedback to your pupils? To evaluate your own teaching success?
- How do you record what these procedures tell you?
- Who uses the information you collect, and for what purpose?
- What direct (primary) evidence do you gather (if any) of what your pupils have experienced and learned?
- What happens to this evidence?
- How do you inform other teachers, or the pupil's next teacher, about the pupils' learning strengths and needs?
- What aspects of your own current practice would you like to change?
- Why?
- What next steps could you take to achieve these changes?

Having thought these through for yourself, the next step might be to share your conclusions with colleagues in your section, or your team, or department, or faculty. If you already work closely with others, you might want to start by going through this list together, or even devise your own questions. The main thing is to work within some common structure, to make your collective discussion easier.

You will probably discover that a fair amount of the decisions you make with your own classroom or team are under your own control: you have devised your own procedures and can change them if necessary by your own decision. There will be other aspects of what you do, however, that are determined by whole-school procedures and requirements. All schools have systems that apply to everyone. Some of these are determined beyond the school: school registers for example are legal documents that have to be completed at certain times and in certain ways. The 1981 Education Act established certain statutory procedures for the identification of children's special educational needs, with which all the schools and LEAs must comply. The 1988 Education Act has added to the list of procedures that schools are legally obliged to follow. Even so, schools do retain a high degree of freedom of action to determine the details of how they arrange internal assessments, for example, or reports, or parents' meetings. The structure and length of the school day has to be within certain statutory parameters, but thereafter the details of times, length of teaching periods and breaks and so on are at the discretion of the school and its governing body, taking due regard of the wishes of the community and of the teachers and their professional associations. As we have seen, the processes of assessment, recording, and reporting are wide-ranging and affect almost every aspect of school life. A whole-school review of its overall procedures will raise many interconnected issues; planning change will in some cases be quite complicated as a result, but not impossibly so.

The next step is to get some 'helicopter vision', looking down at the school as a whole from above or outside it, and make a list of all the procedures for assessing, recording and reporting pupils' learning and development that already exist within your own school. A typical list for an 11 to 18 years secondary school could look like this:

- School 'marking' procedures
- Standardized tests, if they are used
- Internal tests and examinations
- External examinations, and related procedures
- Parental reports
- Records of achievement, processes and documentation
- Data for special needs 'statements'
- Data for the careers service
- Data for parents' evenings/conferences
- References for employers
- Data for admission to further education
- Data for admission to higher education.

Many schools have other systems, for monitoring individual children for example, which you might want to add to this list. Having ascertained the procedures that apply across your school, ask yourselves some critical questions *about each of these*.

- Is the purpose of the procedure clear?
- What is the purpose?
- Who is it for?
- Does what you do match with the purpose, and the needs of the target group?
- Is the information valid, reliable and intelligible?
- Is the procedure cost-effective? — does the quality of the outcome justify the time, energy and resources required to produce it?

- Is the information produced used — by whom and for what purpose?
- Could the cost-effectiveness of the procedure, or the quality of the outcome, be improved? If so, how? What might be the consequences of such change for other parts of the school's operation?

These questions may be fairly basic, but the responses they produce can be fundamental. That is their worth, but it can also be a drawback, as their interconnections make any change appear outfacing. For those of us who like our problems and their solutions to be arranged in easy categories — 'today', 'tomorrow' and 'too hard' — this might be promptly placed on the 'too hard' pile. However, in the current climate, with the current changes facing us, for most schools, no change is not an option. The challenge is to think through the sequence and timing of necessary and desirable change and then take it one step at a time, being aware of the possible constraints and complexities but not letting them paralyse you.

Both the analysis models presented here, at the individual and whole-school level, have the question 'Why?' as a prime requirement. They should raise our awareness, too, of the difference between 'principles' and 'systems' in assessment, and remind us that principles need to be our starting point, to guide us through the labyrinth of administrative possibilities that present themselves and require decisions to be made that are educationally sound rather than just logistically convenient. The discussion of such principles is the starting point for our next whole-school issue.

Developing a Whole-school Policy

As I mentioned earlier, schools have had plenty of experience in developing school policies over the past few years, and may have already developed effective strategies for doing so. The strategy I want to describe here is presented as a suggestion, no more, based on my own experience with several schools, and could be pursued during a school in-service training (INSET) day, given the appropriate planned preparation and follow-up. The preparation in this case could be an ongoing review of current practice, prefaced in turn by some familiarity with the basic principles of assessment outlined in Chapter One. You might want to start an INSET day with some reminders about basic definitions, for example, the differences between norm and criterion referencing, the concept of validity and its implications, or the connection between assessment and teaching and learning.

This exercise is designed to provoke some discussion, and generate some agreed conclusions about the principles that should underpin a school's approach to assessment in its broadest sense, formative as well as summative, process as well as product. It involves the whole staff, senior staff included, divided into groups of between five and seven. The groups need arranging beforehand, to get a good mix of 'specialisms' — either age- or subject-related — and seniority, to give each person the chance of contributing to a well-balanced discussion. Each group is given the same task:

'The system of assessment, recording and reporting in our school should...'.

Discuss and agree a small number (between six and ten) of carefully-worded statements to complete this sentence. You may have to argue about the precise meanings of the word that you use, but that is alright. It's important that you find a consensus within the group, but that does not necessarily mean that everyone agrees with everything. Write down your agreed statements, and then try the next step.

For some, or all, of your 'principles', consider what *evidence* you might expect to see in your school of these principles in action. For example, one of your principles might be 'The system of assessment, recording and reporting in our school should *involve the child as a central part of the process*'. What evidence might you expect to show that this principle was actually operating in your school? A whole range of possibilities might occur to you. For example, the evidence might be that pupils understand the criteria by which their work is assessed; pupils might regularly be involved in self assessment, having received clear guidance of how to do this effectively; pupils might be present at parents' evenings when their progress is discussed and have an active part to play in the process; pupils might provide their personal evaluation of their own progress as a part of the formative reviewing process, or the reporting process, or both. Any or all of these might function as evidence of the principle in practice. Your choice of appropriate evidence would depend on all sorts of considerations, such as the age of the pupils.

You may well find that the discussion about the evidence reveals that you are not entirely happy with the way you have expressed the principle: if so, go back and change the wording. What is important is that the principle and the evidence make sense together, that they are internally consistent. You will probably also discover that different types of evidence emerge. Some of the evidence is tangible, even quantifiable, while other evidence will be more ephemeral or attitudinal, and to find it you would have to check out the views of pupils, or teachers, or parents.

Many teachers faced with this task want to say quite explicitly that the 'systems' should be 'manageable within existing resources levels', or 'avoid unnecessary duplication' or 'be supported by adequate relevant in-service training', all of which are wholly reasonable, but quite difficult to be very specific about. We all know that what may be considered 'manageable' by one teacher might be regarded as quite unmanageable by another. In one respect, this is a theoretical exercise, but in other ways it is certainly not: the principles that emerge should form the basis of the school's policy on assessment, and evidence described could, in turn, become the starting point for developing 'performance indicators' — more about this later. In other words, this is for real: teachers will be discussing and developing principles that they themselves will be centrally involved in implementing in their own classrooms. Rhetoric is not called for here, but what may develop are arguments about values — the values of the individuals, or the school or the education service as a whole. Some people enjoy discussion about values, others find it difficult, but on this occasion the discussion is unavoidable.

Both the quality, and the time requirements, of this discussion can be affected by several factors. The task will be easier and probably more fruitful if you are working in 'mixed' groups, if you have had such 'policy' discussions before in your own teams, if you are all clear about the purpose of this activity, and confident that your views will be listened to. Some groups like to have someone among them who is charged with getting discussion started, keeping everyone on track and making sure that each person has the chance to say what he or she wants to say and that people listen to each other. That may be something you would want to arrange beforehand.

I would suggest that you give yourselves at least an hour on this task, and you might want longer than that. Just before you can come back together again, each group writes up its principles, and the evidence attached to each principle onto a large piece of paper so that it can be clearly read by others. Back in the plenary session, the sheets of paper are displayed round the room, and everyone gets the chance to read everyone else's. If you want to take it one step further, you ask people to write their comments on the sheet as they read, although that can get messy. A simpler alternative is just to tick or star those principles that seem to be particularly significant, or that are expressed very well, and to 'question-mark' those where the meaning is not clear.

When everyone has had the chance to read other peoples' product, whoever is leading the session could ask for brief feedback, group by group, or generally, about how the group tackled the task, what their major disagreements were, or other constructive conclusions they might have arrived at. It should go without saying here, that certain reasonable ground rules need to be accepted in the large group as well as the small, about people responding to each other with a degree of respect, and searching for consensus rather than for opportunities to block it. There is nothing soft or soggy about the attempt to resolve apparently conflicting views: it is a high-level skill, requiring care and energy, and is very worthwhile to create a sound basis on which to build.

The visual display of the groups' conclusions can quickly reveal the degree of commonality that may prevail across the school. People may have chosen different forms of words to express themselves but the same principles may underpin them. It may be possible to identify a few principles that are clearly held in common: these could be the deepest foundation of the policy framework to be built.

The next step, having identified some key principles, could be for the various teams, sections, departments or whatever, to get together to review their own procedures in the light of these principles. If the principle is already accepted, is it actually working? Where is the evidence? What would we need to do to find it? If the principle is not operational, what steps could we take in our own teaching and organization to make it so? If changes are needed, how do we phase these changes to make them manageable?

... people responding to each other with a degree of respect

Writing the School's Assessment Policy

The art gallery of groups' thinking is much too valuable to waste. What is needed now is a few people willing to undertake the job of analysing, collating and synthesizing the groups' efforts into a list of principles, with suggestions about the practical implications of these principles, based on the evidence. This might take a while to produce, and will then need circulating so that all those involved can see and comment upon the result of their joint efforts.

Up to this point, the only group of people involved in considerations of principle have been the teachers themselves. As the school's most important resource, and as the people most centrally involved in making these principles happen, that seems to me to be entirely appropriate. The school's policy on assessment, recording and reporting, however, once developed, will have an impact on groups other than the teachers. The pupils will be affected, both individually and collectively, as will parents, other schools, further-education or training establishments, and even employers. An area that is so central to the school's purpose and function also closely involves the governing body, and the local authority, which has a legal obligation to 'assure quality' in general, and monitor the National Curriculum implementation in particular.

The question now is, how and when should these groups be involved in the development of the school's policy. Even more basic than that, who is the policy actually for? This is not a philosophical question: the answer to it may, *should*, determine the way the policy statement is structured and written, to make sure it is appropriate for its intended audience. Recognition of the range of audiences involved has prompted some schools to produce two versions of their policy — one for fellow professionals, and another for the non-education community, including the pupils themselves, which is both meaningful and accessible. Is this a positive and realistic strategy, or potentially patronizing?

Whatever policy is created, and whatever the mode or structure used to express it, it is likely to include a recognition of the need to monitor, evaluate and where necessary amend the policy, systematically and regularly. We have all come across whole-school policies that may have been relevant at the time when they are written but have since atrophied. Any school policy worthy of the name deserves to be treated as a dynamic rather than a static statement, if the quality it was designed to promote is to be continually assured.

Finding and Using 'Performance Indicators'

As with most of the current jargon, if you take the commonsense meaning of these two words, it can tell you what this is really about. The jargon is just short-hand, and the idea is basically very simple.

So far, we have looked at ways of identifying the key principles that will underpin our school's assessment policy, so there has already been discussion and possibly a consensus about what we mean by 'performance' in achieving an acceptable whole-school approach. To make those principles real and meaningful, we have also tried to identify the evidence that we would expect to find of the principles actually working in the school. The early bits of evidence often appear rather vague: to turn evidence into performance indicators we need to sharpen them up, and make them quite explicit. Performance indicators are criteria for evaluation, in the same way as statements of attainment are criteria for assessment: as such, therefore, they need to be as clear as we can make them.

Assessment is concerned with the quality as well as the quantity of learning, and with attitudes such as student motivation as well as with scores of grades and numbers. The evidence of good assessment will include 'qualitative' as well as 'quantitative' items, and this balance will be found in the performance criteria, by which we establish how effective our principles are. Quantitative items are sometimes easier to check: we count things, and crunch and compare the figures we come up with. Qualitative items are more difficult; we need to ask those concerned for their judgements of the quality, not merely the quantity, of what they have produced or experienced. Add to this the current obsession with quantification, clearly demonstrated in the numbers and levels of the National Curriculum assessment procedures, and the necessary balance of qualitative and quantitative performance indicators will have to be constantly checked.

The key to success in developing meaningful and manageable performance indicators is three-fold. First, never lose sight of the principles that underpin your efforts; second, try to select a small number of the most significant areas of evidence to refine further into performance indicators; third, plan your evaluation strategy with care and creatively to make it cost- and time-effective and get to the heart of the matter. If your evaluation strategy needs to investigate, for example, the effectiveness of pupil self-assessment you might want to check the perception of both students and teachers. Instead of attempting to interview or administer a questionnaire to all the students and all their teachers, take a small and representative sample. Your evaluation will take less time and effort, and will still generate reliable information if it is properly conducted.

Evaluation, like assessment, is most valuable for formative rather than merely summative purposes, by showing what is working well, and indicating where improvements can be made. Performance indicators, therefore, are pointers to further action, and the cycle of planning, delivery and monitoring becomes a spiral, not just a straight line. There is room here for some really creative thinking: some schools have involved interested members of the governing body in the evaluation of qualitative performance indicators, such as interviewing a sample of students, teachers or even parents about the achievement of some of the school's stated aims and principles. By being closely involved in gathering information from those directly involved, governors can gain invaluable insight into the educative process, which, in turn, helps them to understand the issues they are called upon to deal with. In other schools, implementation of records of achievement has brought with it an accreditation process, by which the school's procedures are monitored by the external accrediting body and its representatives. Here too, existing systems can provide feedback within an agreed framework of performance criteria. At the levels of the individual student, a process of recording achievement, in which student and tutor discuss the student's experience, learning and targets in some depth twice or three time a year, can play a central part in the qualitative evaluation strategy of the school.

Managing Cross-curricular Assessment

Here, as elsewhere in this book, we have to remind ourselves that the basic structures of our thinking about assessment have been around for decades, but have recently been brought into sharper ·focus by the arrival of the National Curriculum, which was, in turn, a feature of the 1988 Education Act. Section One of the Act says many of the things that we would wish to hear about the broad child-centred purposes of education and the comprehensive multi-dimensional nature of children's opportunities for learning and personal development. Curiously perhaps, the National Curriculum was originally described largely in terms of core and foundation 'subjects', with the cross-curricular implications added later. This broader-based discussion about learning and development can be hampered by a plethora of potentially confusing terminology — core skills, cross-curricular skills, themes, threads, and so on. For the sake of ease, I shall take the definitions presented to us by the National Curriculum Council (NCC) in *Curriculum Guidance Three: The Whole Curriculum* and add one of my own. Cross-curricular 'dimensions, skills and themes' have been offered by the NCC; cross-curricular overlap between core and foundation subjects is where I would like to start.

Handling National Curriculum Subject Overlap

It cannot be said too often that the ten National Curriculum core and foundation subjects are merely a vehicle for describing the statutory programmes of study and attainment targets, produced by subject teams under the auspices of the NCC, and sometimes without reference to each other. This subject-specific presentation does not and cannot dictate the means whereby we present the required curriculum to our pupils. It is the responsibility of the school *as a whole* to deliver and assess the National Curriculum. Attainment levels need to be monitored in the school by the end of each Key Stage but the evidence on which such judgements are based is not the exclusive responsibility of any one teacher, team or department. This is self-evident in a primary school where the class teacher is responsible for all the statutory areas of learning but needs careful thought in those secondary schools that are organized on subject-departmental lines. It is there where we need to think through the implications of the suggestion from the NCC that we can ignore all the subject labels on programmes of study and attainment targets, if we wish, mix them up and arrange them in whatever packages of curriculum we wish to devise in the best interests of our pupils in each unique community. The 'what' is prescribed: the 'how' is at the discretion of the school.

As the National Curriculum details have unfolded, subject by subject, the pace of development has often inhibited secondary specialists from looking beyond their own subject boundaries. Coming to terms with the 'ring-binders' containing statutory orders for each subject has made sufficient demands on teachers' time and energy. Nevertheless, as the dust begins to clear, it is obvious that cross-subject overlap exists, and in ways that we might not have predicted. We might not have foreseen the commonalities in certain approaches between English and technology, for example, whereas the overlap between science and technology, or science and geography was more expected.

Some schools have already begun the process of curriculum mapping, to identify and manage the overlap in teaching terms, but the management of assessment and record-keeping in these areas presents some interesting challenges. If we accept the integral connection between teaching, learning and assessment, it follows that the teachers who teach a particular content area should also be responsible for assessing it. Having the earth science taught by the scientists and assessed by the geographers, or *vice versa* makes no sense at all, and would probably render the assessment unreliable in the process.

Assessment follows teaching, therefore, but what about those areas for which both teaching, learning and assessment opportunities abound all over the curriculum. The most obvious example is English, where the five attainment targets — 'Speaking and Listening', 'Reading', 'Writing', 'Spelling' and 'Handwriting' could *theoretically* be assessed by the teachers of science, technology, history, geography, and others, as well as by English teachers. As the framework of attainment targets in all areas unfolds, other examples of this theoretical possibility will also be found.

The successful management of curriculum overlap is one of the keys to National Curriculum implementation, and could help markedly in reducing assessment overload, but the assessment process in this situation needs to be approached with care. Teacher assessment of the given criteria of the National Curriculum structure must be underpinned by internal standardization procedures in order to be reliable, that is, to be fair to the pupils. This is not an unfamiliar idea for those teachers who have been involved in external examinations, particularly with the onset of the GCSE. What is new, however, is the idea of teachers making reliable assessment judgements of areas normally considered to be outside their own subject parameters. Although much very significant speaking and listening has always been observable in science and technology activities, for example, these have not generally been used for assessment purposes, and the teachers concerned will therefore not have had experience of sharing and standardizing their expectations. Much has been learned by their colleagues in the English departments, but they may not yet have introduced other teachers to the practicalities of oral assessment.

Without such standardization, which could be quite time-consuming to begin with because of the ephemeral nature of some of the evidence, the judgements of non-English teachers could be deemed unreliable and the quality of overall Teacher Assessment in the school could be affected. Other areas could cause difficulty too, if assessment of particular criteria is spread too widely, too fast. The assessment of written work raises issues about the practice of re-drafting, levels of teacher intervention, and acceptable levels of parental support and encouragement where work is taken home.

The problems are resolvable but would require considerable thought, training, practice and close cross-subject collaboration.

Some secondary schools have already seen the exciting possibilities in managing both the presentation and assessment of the National Curriculum in ways that are not only cost-effective by avoiding duplication of teacher time and effort, but also educationally sound, in reflecting the reality of children's learning, which does not develop in discrete subject-based chunks as they move through school. Making connections across all areas of learning could become a reality with positive benefits for both teachers and learners but only if the rigour and quality of what we do is maintained.

Cross-curricular Dimensions

The NCC's explanation for this term involves two major areas: 'providing equal opportunities for all pupils', and 'a recognition that preparation for adult life in a multicultural society is relevant to all pupils'. The assessment implications may not immediately strike you but they are in fact fundamental. We are expected in schools to make our assessment of each child, individually, as accurate as we can, against the background of specific common criteria. In trying to get as close as we can to the reality of each child's learning and attainment, we need to take account of each child's uniqueness, so far as we are able to. The child's language skills, physical abilities, cultural experience, all have a bearing not only on what is taught and learned, but also on the child's means of articulating and demonstrating that learning to us. It requires professional care and skill to handle the unique variables represented in each of our pupils and make what we feel to be a fair and accurate judgement. If we achieve it, however, the cause of equal opportunity and equal access to learning and recognition will have been enhanced: good assessment and equal-opportunity issues go hand in hand.

Cross-curricular Skills

Ever since the NCC's '*Curriculum Guidance Three, The Whole Curriculum*' was issued in 1989, the developments have continued and the terminology has changed too. Nevertheless, beneath new titles the same basic commonsense reality exists. The fact is, always has been and always will be, that children, as they learn, develop and demonstrate skills that cut across the relatively artificial boundaries of subjects, areas of experience or whatever we are calling them this year. The list of these skills may change slightly from era to era, in line with technological development and societal expectation, but much of it remains the same. The NCC list of cross-curricular skills contains:

- Communication
- Numeracy
- Study
- Problem solving
- Personal and social
- Information technology

Similar lists of identified skills have been around for decades. Surely, previous experience of handling the assessment and recording of these skills should help us. We should certainly hope so, as much previous experience, in Scotland, in the English and Welsh Records of Achievement pilot schemes and in countless individual schools has often produced lessons from which we can learn. From my own experience in this field over the past decade, let me outline a scenario to be avoided if possible, and an alternative that seems to offer greater hope.

Assessing Cross-curricular Skills: The Story so Far...

To appreciate fully the irony of the development I am about to describe, take your mind back to the 'good old days' in the secondary school when most of us taught 'subjects'. We knew where we stood: 'subject' meant a clear knowledge base, and we maintained a respectful distance from colleagues whose knowledge base was different from ours. If the boundaries did overlap, only the most perceptive child would notice. If he or she had the impertinence to point out, 'But we've done this before', the reply was swift, 'Well this time you're doing it properly'. Life was simple.

The onset of curriculum review in the 1970s began to erode this sense of security. We were asked to analyse our subject offerings in terms of their 'concepts, skills and attitudes'. This done, we discovered that these were unlikely to be exclusive to our own subjects. Lists from different subject areas were collated and compared.

The conclusion was inescapable; cross-curricular skills did exist, and they could be identified and listed, which they promptly were.

So far so good, but the next steps were critical. Did every teacher now have to assess, record and report each of these skills? Some schools and systems said 'yes', and the paper mountain grew as we all struggled to produce judgements on 'numeracy', or 'spatial awareness' and even on occasions specific personal skills like 'self-confidence' or 'reliability'. Much angst resulted. On what basis could or should we judge another human being's reliability? What if 'numeracy' did not appear to happen naturally in my English lesson? Did I have to contrive to get some numbers in?

In some schools, for all sorts of reasons, the drive towards cross-curricular assessment was allowed to slacken. Deals were struck between subject-specialists. Oracy was handed back to the English teachers (with much relief on all sides) and numeracy was welcomed home by the mathematicians. By a slow but inexorable process, skills returned to their most obvious 'landlords'. In other schools, however, the drive for uniformity from the top was strong. 'Yes, every teacher should assess everything whether this was a comfortable business or not.' All teachers continued to produce assessments of all the identified skills, often in terms of a letter grade or number, which were sometimes (but not always) related to a 'descriptor' denoting the level or quality of the particular skill. Little or no standardizing of these judgements took place between teachers. The contexts within which the skills were demonstrated were not recorded. The result was a plethora of de-contextualized grades or comments, and too many of them to be easily managed for summative purposes.

At this point, computer data banks were sometimes called in to help manage and collate the data; otherwise simpler aggregated or average grades were produced by hand. In other schools again, all the data was passed to the pupil's tutor, who combined an average view of the results in each skill area with his or her own knowledge of the pupil to produce a summative statement for reporting purposes.

In all of these cases, whether the judgement was derived from cross-curricular evidence or not, the final result was a generalized grade or comment, referring to the skill but not the contexts in which it was developed and demonstrated. These grades and comments were then offered to people not involved in the original learning experiences such as parents, further trainers or employers, and the questions began. 'What do these grades and statements really mean? Come to that, what does 'problem-solving' mean? Were the 'problems' technological, ethical, sociological or mathematical? Where was the evidence to support these judgements, some of which might be about the personal qualities of the child as a child, not as a learner in school?' Parents might have been puzzled, perhaps even annoyed, that this process of judgement of personal skills and qualities seemed to be taking place without reference to them.

After all the time, effort and resources harnessed to arrive at these judgements, serious doubt could be cast on their validity, reliability, meaning and usefulness. Was it all worth it? Schools' own experiences, the reaction of employers, and sometimes the reaction of the pupils themselves, seemed to indicate that this approach to cross-curricular assessment left something to be desired. Is there another way through, simpler, less-expensive, more meaningful, less ambitious but more effective? Perhaps.

Cross-curricular Learning: Evidence in Context

An alternative procedure exists; it developed slowly as the inadequacies of the first models became clear. The starting point is familiar. Cross-curricular skills are identified, and 'mapped' or recognized in those learning areas where they arise. Teachers and pupils together clarify and become aware of them, and of their relevance to learning both at school and beyond. Pupils as well as teachers are alerted to look for and recognize examples of the skills where they are used.

If a particular activity or experience provides illuminating evidence of any or some of these skills, it is noted, as concisely as possible, and forms part of the pupil's classroom-based reviewing process. If there is tangible evidence, beyond the brief description of the context and achievement, then that could be retained too, dated and annotated, in the pupil's portfolio. Only selected and significant examples are kept: the pupils themselves become initiators of this process as they become more confident, although they may need more support in the early stages.

Periodically, perhaps twice during each school year, the pupil meets for 20 minutes or so with his or her review tutor, and together they review the evidence of experience and learning since they last met, check whether earlier targets have been reached and agree a small number of targets for the future. These could relate to particular subject areas, or to more general cross-curricular or extra-curricular areas. Decisions are made about the evidence to be taken forward into the following year, and what can now be removed from the portfolio because it has since been subsumed in further achievement, or is no longer relevant to the current stage of the pupil's development. The shelf-life of the evidence may be quite short.

During the early months of the pupil's final year of compulsory schooling, when the procedures to compile the summative statements in the record of achievement begin, the young person and the tutor select the evidence, in context, that best illustrates some or all of the cross-curricular skills they have been discussing. These items form part of the final record, or of the portfolio of selected evidence that accompanies it. Grades and scores on cross-curricular skills have been abandoned as impractical, unreliable and largely meaningless. Meaning can be derived more easily by looking at the description of attainment in context. The reader (the employer, the admission tutor or 'gate-keeper') considers the relevance or potential transferability of the skill concerned. If receivers are only interested in the cruder, more generalized 'level' of the young person in terms of subject attainment, the National Curriculum levels or GCSE grades within the records of achievement will offer such information.

The process of periodic review undertaken by the pupil and the tutor together — for which both will have received some basic training — will itself provide opportunity for monitoring the pupil's overall learning and development. Curriculum monitoring is not merely a paper exercise concerned with input: it can now focus on what the young person takes out of the curriculum, how learning in different parts of the school and beyond the school are related to each other.

Technically speaking, defining assessment in its narrowest sense, describing the evidence in context of cross-curricular skill may not be a form of assessment. It may not satisfy those who feel that the assessment should always produce a quantifiable result. The issues here are contentious. What do you think?

Cross-curricular Themes

Five cross-curricular themes have been identified by the National Curriculum Council:

- Economic and industrial understanding
- Careers education and guidance
- Health education
- Education for citizenship
- Environmental education.

Each of these has been the subject of a booklet in the *Curriculum Guidance* series, in which the area is defined, exemplified and related to other parts of the National Curriculum framework. The themes are non-statutory, although some of them reflect current teaching practice of high quality and effectiveness. No attempt has been made to identify detailed and specific criteria for assessment in the form of statements of attainment or attainment targets. Standard Assessment Tasks based on these themes are not envisaged. The assessment of them, therefore, is not part of the statutory requirement, but some schools may still want to assess them as a means of recognizing their importance and parity with other areas of the National Curriculum in which assessment is a requirement.

Depending on how themes are to be delivered in a school, as discrete areas, as strands within National Curriculum subject teaching, or by any other model that suits the school, the assessment issue will be affected by many of the considerations we have already encountered. If themes are integrated into teaching in different areas of the school, unstandardized judgement is meaningless. Just as the themes themselves only become clear through exemplification, so judgements about them essentially need context to make them meaningful. De-contextualized, unstandardized grades or comments are simply not worth producing. The most satisfactory decision may be not to assess themes in any formal sense, but to incorporate them into the 'evidence in context' part of the record of achievement procedure.

Progression

All educators, in each phase of the education service from nursery schools to higher and adult education, aim to ensure that learning is a continual process. Some changes in the learning environment from one phase to the next are both inevitable and welcome as different phases respond to the developing needs of learners, but these changes should be supportive of progress and never damaging to it. Right through the service, all of us share a responsibility to ensure that learning experience, strengths and needs are recognized, clearly communicated and met. A first essential for effective progression is mutual respect and trust between the different teams of educators. These teams largely stay together and in one place: it is the learner who moves from one team to the next. To that extent, therefore, the learner him or herself is the vehicle of his or her own progression. Our strategies must both enable and enhance that process.

This is the accepted rhetoric of progression, but what can we do to make it actually happen? Firstly, we need to liaise as carefully as we can, to see and understand for ourselves the actual learning experience of children and young people before they reach us, and when they move on to the next learning environment. So far as the logistics of such an exercise will allow, teachers need to visit each other's institutions, nursery to reception and *vice versa*, infant to junior and *vice versa*, junior to secondary and *vice versa*, and so on. No matter what information passes between us on paper, we only really understand it when we can visualize the context from which that information has derived.

Secondly, and frequently achieved already, we enable children to see for themselves the next learning environment as they approach transition. Children and young people have very natural anxieties about what may lie in store for them as they move from one school to the next, and those anxieties usually centre on the social experience not just the academic. Year Six children for example, where transition takes place at 11-plus years, worry every year about the change from being the eldest, and the biggest, in a relatively small building, to being the youngest and smallest in a much larger space. Rumours about 'rites of passage' abound: bullying or intimidation, or getting lost, loom very large in the minds of some children, particularly those who are less selfconfident or mature for their age. In 11-plus transfer systems, for example, strategies include secondary age children visiting and doing work experience in the local primary schools, Year Six children coming to the secondary school not just to look around, but to attend functions, to use some specialist facilities, to spend days there working on a special project and getting used to larger people around them. The children can familiarize themselves with the playground, the dining rooms, even the toilets and less well-supervised areas where their worst fears seem to lurk.

Many schools prepare for and welcome their intake every year by displays of their work, encouraging the children themselves to bring and show examples of what they have done in recent months, attaching older children to the newcomers to 'mind' and support them, offering a structured 'induction' programme to familiarize children as quickly as possible with the building and all the people who work in it, non-teaching as well as teaching staff. All these strategies are based on the sound common sense that children who are very anxious find learning difficult. Reduce the anxieties and the learning threads can be picked up fast and effectively. The best pastoral care is preventative, not curative.

Effective progression also has major implications for the structures of learning, such as timetables and movement from room to room, and how individual classrooms are managed. Between primary and secondary schooling there can be major differences for children in what they actually do at school. Instead of being mostly with one teacher in one room, they find themselves encountering ten or even more teachers in a week, moving from one specialist area to another carrying books and equipment with them, with a more fragmented day than they may have had before. Some are ready for such a change, and others are not. Some schools try to ease the change more gradually by reducing the number of teachers and room changes the incoming children are exposed to. Hence the ideas of Year Seven 'foundation courses', where children experience some parts of their more differentiated 'subject-based' curriculum in larger blocks, with one teacher covering several areas. The 'pros' and 'cons' of such arrangements have been well-rehearsed, but they are certainly worth consideration if they have the potential to ease progression and thereby improve children's learning. The subject-specific nature of National Curriculum documentation makes no real difference here: it is the responsibility of the school to deliver the broad and balanced curriculum described in part in the National Curriculum. To do so, the school can choose whatever methods of delivery it wishes, the essential purpose being to promote children's learning as effectively as possible. What are your views on all this?

Record-keeping and Progression

Quite deliberately so far I have made no mention of the documentation of progression, the records kept by teachers to pass on information about children to the next school, or from one teacher to the next. The content, structure, timing and use made of such records is often a bone of contention between different phases of the service. Sometimes discussion about progression seems to focus too much on the records to the neglect of other progression strategies I have already referred to. Looking at records alone produces an almost insoluble dilemma. Those presenting children to the next school want to reflect the range and depth of what they know about the children, but are daunted by the task of writing it all down. Those receiving children may not be able to handle a large quantity of specific information. Even if they are able to read and absorb it, they may not be sure how to use what they have learned.

The critical dilemma for the receiving school is this: can the Year Seven curriculum (or whichever year is the new intake) be made responsive enough to accommodate the specific identified needs of our new intake? To put it simply, and to risk unfairness to the professionalism of many secondary school teachers, the less we know about each child's previous experience, strengths and needs, the less responsive we need to be. In schools that draw from a large number of 'feeder' schools, the dilemma is exacerbated, at least until the cohering impact of the National Curriculum is felt right through the 5 to 16 years age range. There is no question that planning to be responsive to individual children's needs is hard work and a challenge to our capacity to manage, support and resource the curriculum. In some schools, but thankfully a decreasing number, the traditional solution to the dilemma has been a *post facto* rationalization called 'letting children make a fresh start'. Here again we can debate the 'pros' and 'cons'. In terms of behaviour and forming positive relationships, a fresh start may be just what some children need; but if fresh start means ignoring their previous learning and experience and providing that which incidentally suits the teachers rather than the children, progression is at risk.

The issues here are quite complex, and vary slightly from one stage of transfer to the next, and it is therefore essential to go back each time to the question 'What strategies will best fulfil the fundamental purpose of enhancing learning and personal development?' and then do our best, with all the constraints of time and resources, to deliver those strategies.

Assessment and records do have a place in progression strategies but their importance needs to be qualified. Assessments made and communicated to another school or teacher are only useful if the criteria that underpin the assessment are shared and understood. Reading ages, for example, as determined by standardized tests, have only ever been useful if we know which reading test was used. With the onset of the National Curriculum assessment this confusion might resolve itself. Discussions about standardizing between teachers on either side of an institutional divide will help enormously too.

Assessments and records of what children have achieved cannot and should not be treated as predictive of what children can and will achieve. Schools are sometimes tempted to question the accuracy of previous school records because the child seems unable to reproduce that level of attainment in the new environment. Circumstances do have an impact on any learner's capacity to demonstrate what he or she can do: it could be expected therefore that a 6-week break followed by a marked change in almost every aspect of the learning environment (*e.g.* place, people, relationships and expectations) will reduce temporarily the 'performance' of the child, without in any way undermining the validity of the previous judgements that have been made. Transfer records, however they are structured, should be accepted and used for what they are: reflections of the professional judgements of colleagues who have experienced children in a different environment over an extended period. They can tell us a great deal about *how* children learn, what motivates them, what special talents, strengths and needs they have on which the next school can build. De-contextualized codes or non-specific aggregated statements about the child's attainment all take time to decide and record, and remain of very limited formative value to the next teacher or school. All records, secondary evidence of children's learning, are greatly enhanced by accompanying examples of primary evidence to illuminate and exemplify the records, and can be quickly absorbed by a fellow educator.

Chapter Six:
Forward to Fundamentals

'Forward to fundamentals': I am grateful to whoever first coined this phrase, as it encapsulates so neatly my purpose for writing this book. My constant attempt has been to de-mystify the process of assessment, to integrate it into teaching, learning and whole-school organization, and to emphasize its prime purpose of enhancing the development of children and young people as they pass through the education service into their adult lives.

Of all the areas for review and development suggested in the preceding chapters, I would draw out two to re-emphasize and exemplify. If these two were pursued as the highest priority by teachers and schools, many of the initiatives and projects that descend on us would be delivered without an acronym in sight.

My two priorities would be:

- Clear, shared learning targets, and
- Systematic encouragement of the self-awareness and self-respect of our children and young people.

Clear, Shared Learning Targets

Underpinning the pursuit of this aim is the belief, which most of us would accept without question, that learners of any age learn more effectively if they understand what it is that they are aiming at. The role of teacher, therefore is to find the means of communicating to each learner not only the ultimate goal but also the steps by which the goal must be reached. The number and height of the steps will vary from learner to learner. Quite possibly, the route followed by these steps will vary too, as each learner recognizes different features of the landscape and makes choices along the way, without losing sight of the final destination. The teacher, who knows most if not all routes well, has a role in making each step within the extended stride or grasp of the learner, and in doing what he or she can to provide the map, and to encourage and support.

In the current climate, and within the existing parameters of time, energy and resources, what can teachers and learners do to establish clear, shared, learning objectives? For a start, we need to find a balance between the entirely reactive role, when 'OK, children what shall we do today?' is not a rhetorical question but means that you have no teaching plan at all, and the curriculum plan that is so tight and inflexible that there is no chance of adapting it to the needs and interests of individual children. The overall topic or lesson plan is clear in your mind but there is still room for the children's particular questions and expectations to be gathered and then met.

... the curriculum plan that is so tight and inflexible that there is no chance of adapting it to the needs...of...children...

If the framework of teaching and assessment is largely determined by National Curriculum Programmes of Study and Attainment Targets, then these need to be shared with learners as well. This is not easy, as they were certainly not written for either pupils or their parents. Many teachers both primary and secondary have already realized the possible benefits of 'translating' National Curriculum documentation into language and structures accessible to their pupils. 'Child-speak' versions can be found all over the country, with teachers often collaborating to share the work. On top of all the other pressing requirements, this is a considerable task but one that could certainly pay off in time, as both children and parents are better able to understand the matrix of targets and levels.

Once learning targets, within the National Curriculum framework and beyond it, are clarified and shared, learners as well as teachers can be involved in monitoring and recording where those targets have been met, and where to go next. Other areas of pupil involvement also open up once the aim of the exercise is clear. Children and young people can identify how the classroom and resources need to be managed to best meet those targets, and can take some responsibility themselves in this respect. If evidence of learning is being sought, pupils can be part of that search, among their own work and also, through group or peer assessment, identifying evidence of learning in the work of others. The learning criteria, once understood, can be internalized by learners so that they can become real partners in the teaching process.

Once learning targets are determined, shared and used formatively in the classroom a host of possibilities opens up, which some teachers welcome and others find hard to accept. Underpinning some of the anxiety, which is often unstated, is a concern that classroom control may be lost if the teachers share with children the details of what is to be done and how. In this scenario, power over the learning environment is seen as a finite commodity: if it is shared, then the teacher will lose. The experience of others would seem to tell us that where control is shared, the teacher gains as much as the pupils, as the overall involvement in learning rises. The only way to check for yourself is to take a small step and see what happens.

Self-awareness and Self-respect

For those who still regard education as clearly divisible into 'academic' and 'pastoral' with little overlap between the two, a division between this section and the last may seem to reinforce that divide. Closer reading under the heading of clear, shared learning targets reveals that some of the principles of good personal and social education, such as pupils' involvement, responsibilities and choices, have emerged in classroom or 'subject' learning. Unsurprisingly, therefore, any consideration of the importance of self-awareness and self-respect cannot be parcelled up as a tutorial or pastoral or PSE matter: the academic/pastoral divide never did reflect the reality of how children learn and develop, and never will. For most teachers this is self-evident, but I still meet some who insist that they teach a subject, not children.

This is not the place to debate the 'pros' and 'cons' of various models of delivering personal and social education, within or beyond a tutorial programme. Whatever the structures, children need, throughout their education, opportunities to become aware of their own strengths, needs, talents and aspirations. To do so they need to recognize the breadth of their own experience within and beyond school, to connect the various areas of learning and to reflect on all this periodically, helped by an adult, and their peers as well if the peer atmosphere is supportive and comfortable. The 'tutorial' review process at the heart of recording achievement is the obvious means for the systematic personal reflection and target-setting. Maybe twice during each school year, for perhaps 15 to 20 minutes, the young person meets with his or her tutor, to review the evidence of learning and development gathered since they last talked in depth, checking whether the personal targets established last time have been met, deciding targets for the following months.

All sorts of implications spring from this opportunity. The sheer logistics of time, numbers, spaces, preparation, storage of evidence, transferring evidence from each class teacher to tutor all need thinking through. The way through the problem may involve a tutorial reviewing role for every member of staff, finding time on the timetable, or by slight adjustments in the school day. All these arrangements need care if they are to be established effectively. Teachers and students may need training and support to be clear about the purposes and skills involved, how to make best use of the time they have together, and how to develop a summary as part of the annual or end-of-school Record of Achievement.

Where schools manage to put in place systematic sharing of learning objectives, close involvement of students in learning and assessment and the tutorial review to add personal target-setting and synthesize the whole, the motivation of students can rise markedly, and with it their performance, academic as well as personal, measurable and unmeasurable.

The Stories of Two Children: Anne and Imtiaz

To illustrate what impact these principles and strategies could have on the learning and development of young people in our schools, I offer two examples that draw on a range of existing practice. All the strategies mentioned are both workable and working, and seem a fitting way to end a book about assessment, reaffirming as our central concern the children and young people themselves.

Anne

Anne attends a nursery attached to the local primary school. Although some of the activities are organized by the teachers and assistants, for some parts of the day, Anne and her friends are encouraged to choose and plan their own activities. Like the other children, Anne has a special achievement bag, in which she puts anything that she has drawn, or written, or even something she has made or a photograph of it, to show her parents. Each week the children talk with their teacher about what is in their bags. They look at each others items and explain what they like about their own or each other's work.

When the time comes to move into the reception class, Anne chooses a few things to show her new teacher. The nursery class teacher has chosen some things too, to help the next teacher understand how Anne is learning. These include pictures of Mummy, one drawn when Anne started in the nursery at the age of 3 years, one when she was 4, and one just before she left the nursery. Each picture is dated, so that the Reception class teacher can put them side by side, and see how Anne's perception of her mother, and her ability to represent it, has changed over time. Previously the nursery class teacher used to make very detailed records, which the reception class teacher did not have time to read carefully for every child. Now the records are less-detailed and shorter, and the child's own evidence of learning is used as a fast and meaningful way of communicating between one teacher and the next.

In the primary school, the practice of choosing items of work to keep goes on, but now the teachers use folders to keep the children's work in, and there's a special form to indicate when the work was done, from what activity it arose, and why it has been chosen. The children learn to complete these forms themselves as they get older. Each week, the teacher spends a few minutes with one of the children to go through what is in the folder, to take out items that have been replaced by others, and to talk about one thing the child could do to improve his or her work. When it was Anne's turn, she took out some written work she had done 6 months before, realized how much better she was forming her letters now, and agreed with her teacher that she needed to concentrate on full stops and capital letters to improve her written work. Anne brings in some things from home to add to her folder: she is learning to ride, and she brings in a photograph of herself on horseback. She also keeps a list of what she does in Brownies, including a description of the camp they go to each year.

When she moves from the infants to the junior building across the playground, she takes with her a selection of items from her folder, to show her next teacher. When her teacher prepares the annual report about Anne's progress, Anne writes a few sentences herself about what she feels most proud of over the past year, and what she wants to concentrate on next. A few days before her parents come in to see the teacher, she takes home her folder, so that her parents can have a look at it, and talk it through with the teacher when they come in.

Towards the end of Year Six, after summer half-term, Anne's class starts a project that involves going to do some work in the local comprehensive school. Nearly all Anne's classmates will go to this school because the others are a long bus ride away. The teachers from the junior school and the Year Seven team at the high school have planned this project between them, to start in June, and then carry on into Year Seven in September. At the end of it, there will be a big display of their work in the school entrance hall. Anne takes her own folder of work with her too, while her teacher sends through the more-detailed record of Anne's attainment levels in each part of the National Curriculum.

When she moves across into the high school, Anne has to cope with a much bigger building, but she knows her way around because of the time she spent there during the previous term. She stays with the same group of children for most of her lessons, and sees one of her teachers for a third of each week, who teaches a combined English, religious education and humanities course. In Year Eight, she will see more teachers each week than she does in Year Seven.

During the time she was working on her project in the high school, at the end of Year Six, she met her review tutor for the first time. This was a teacher who has special responsibility for a group of students spread through the various year groups of the school. Three other of Anne's friends in Year Seven are in the same review group, and they meet their review tutor once each half-term, on a Tuesday when school finishes 20 minutes early. At the start of Year Seven their tutor actually saw them twice during the first half-term, just to check they were settling down all right, to look at the work they had been doing and to help them decide what to focus on next. They each received a new folder too, and now work from all subject lessons could be chosen, dated, annotated briefly to say why it had been selected, and passed on to the tutor to become a part of the next review. All Anne's teachers build some sort of reviewing into their lessons, but all in different ways and at different times so it does not get boring or repetitive.

Anne finds this occasional overall review with her tutor very useful, as it helps her to make connections between what she learns in different areas of the school and to recognize how much she learns outside school too. Her folder represents a rounded view of her, not just subject learning, and her tutor is sometimes able to help her with a problem she may be having. Once or twice she has asked to see her tutor alone, and they have talked about something in confidence, which was not recorded on the brief review and target sheet they complete during each review. Her tutor listened as she explained the particular problem she was having at home, and suggested that Anne went to the Head of House about it, as she was specially trained to deal with problems like that.

Each year Anne's parents come to a 'conference' with Anne and her review tutor. Together they look through Anne's folder, which reflects both what Anne has achieved during the year and those areas where she is having difficulties that need to be focused on in the future. They agree what each of them can do to help overcome the main difficulties they have identified. If Anne's parents want to see a particular subject teacher, they make an appointment to come in and do so. In Year Nine, Anne and her review tutor concentrate on decisions about Anne's choices and courses for Key Stage Four. Anne is well used to the process of reflecting on her own strengths and needs, and has learned to make decisions about things that are important to her. During Year Ten she sees her review tutor on her own, and they talk about the drafting of summative statements, which will form part of the Record of Achievement she will use in Year Eleven to help find the right training or job. Her folder, or portfolio, as it is now called, contains her work-experience report, and a statement about the babysitting she does regularly for a neighbour.

Anne wants to go to the local college of further education (FE) to do an electronics course, and she needs her portfolio properly organized and ready for her interview before Easter in Year Eleven. Some other of her friends, who are staying on into the sixth form do not need their portfolios finalized until later in the year so the tutor can spread her effort over a longer period of time. Anne and her friends are quite clear about the purpose of their regular review, and they have spent time in PSE too talking about self-presentation and interviewing, so they are mostly able to drive the process themselves. Each of them drafts a personal statement on a word-processor so that if they do want to make changes or additions as they progress through Year Eleven it is not too difficult to do so. If someone wants to see a sample of their handwriting, they can ask for it, but the record of achievement final statements present factual information and evidence as clearly as possible, and printing is best for this purpose.

Anne attaches a copy of her personal statement to the application form for the FE college, and she takes her portfolio with her to the interview. As preparation for her interview, she decides which items of evidence will be of particular interest to the college, and highlights these. She decides to remove one or two items from her portfolio that are more personal and she does not want to share. These are important for her and her family and will stay at home.

The evidence in Anne's portfolio helps her to present examples of what she has learned at school. The process of regular reflection, identifying strengths, needs and targets, and being able to articulate them, which she has been involved in over several years, enables her to both present herself and to ask the questions that are important in her choice of training. When she starts work on her new course at the college she is able to organize herself well, meet deadlines, ask for the help she needs and make decisions about her first job. When she finds, applies for and interviews for this job all the same skills and experience help her again. As her new employer says, the 'product' of the process she has followed is not just the record and evidence she carries with her, but herself — clear, forward-looking, prepared for her working and adult life. Even the appraisal system that operates in the company she joins is very familiar to her.

Imtiaz

Imtiaz does not go to a nursery school, so his first contact with teachers and school is in the reception class in the First Year. The school asks to see all the parents of new children, and also has a brief questionnaire, which Imtiaz's parents fill in, to help the school find out more about him and how he is developing. Many of the parents who send their children to this school speak Urdu. They have received information about the school in Urdu as well as English, and can reply to the questionnaire in Urdu if they find it easier. The questionnaire asks for information about the usual things, emergency contacts, special health or diet, numbers in the family and so on, but it also asks more open questions about what is special about the child, what concerns the parents may have, even what makes them laugh about him. It helps the teachers to get a feel for the child as they begin to work together.

During Key Stage One, in this school like the one Anne goes to, the children are involved right from the start in talking about their work, what they like and dislike about what they do. Sometimes the teacher is involved in the discussion, but sometimes the children talk to each other, in pairs about their reading, or in the group working together on a technology project or the science activity they are busy with. Imtiaz, like Anne, has a folder in which he and his teacher put items from time to time, dated and annotated, which the teacher refers to when she completes the attainment record or profile as Imtiaz progresses through the school. Towards the end of each year, Imtiaz's next teacher has a good look through the folders of the children she will take next year, so that she can begin to plan to meet their individual needs. Imtiaz learns to swim, and brings in to school the certificates that he receives. Some of the things he does at home could be part of his portfolio, but he chooses not to share them at school at the moment. His parents have been told about the portfolio of achievement that he has at school. They understand that its purpose is to recognize and encourage Imtiaz's personal development as well as his school learning, and that the school does not wish to pry into the home life of the family. When Imtiaz begins to learn Urdu in a class organized at the Mosque, he decides to add something about that to his portfolio, and his teacher talks to him about this. This part of his learning does not take place at school, but is an important part of his learning life, and can be represented in his portfolio.

At the age of 9 years, Imtiaz moves from his first school to the middle school. He is half way through Key Stage Two at this stage, and the records of his learning experience and attainment, as well as the evidence in his portfolio, are essential for the middle school, to pick up as quickly as possible and take him on through the Key Stage Two programmes of study. The examples of his number work in the portfolio tell his Year Five teacher more about the difficulties he is experiencing than the estimates of target levels that come through on his attainment record. Much of the evidence in the portfolio illustrates what Imtiaz is good at, but he understands that the next teacher has to see what he is having difficulty with so that she can help him make progress.

For a year or two in the middle school Imtiaz works for most of the week with his class teacher, but gradually different teachers take on different subject areas, and occasionally a technology teacher from the upper school comes in to let them have a go with some resources which the middle school does not have. In Technology, the children are all involved in keeping records of their own progress in their projects. They learn to follow the problem-solving process that lies at the heart of the subject, and get used to the various stages involved.

As the number of teachers Imtiaz sees each week increases, he begins to recognize that each one has a different way of sharing learning targets with the class, but whatever the different systems are they are all based on the same idea. Imtiaz likes to know what is expected of him, and the basis on which his work will be assessed. He also likes the chance he gets to suggest how these targets might be best reached, within the constraints of space and resources that the teacher has explained to him. To help him make connections across his learning, he has a tutor who sees him twice each year, to review the range of his learning within and beyond the school. At parents' evenings, Imtiaz comes along too. There is always someone at hand who speaks Urdu, who can help to explain things if the family is not comfortable using English. In the classroom too the children sometimes talk in Urdu to each other, and when the SATs came along in Year Six, some of the children were given instructions about the task in their home language, to make sure that they understood properly what they were being asked to do.

Imtiaz transfers to upper school at the end of Year Eight, with only one year of Key Stage Three left. The record of teaching and learning in Year Seven and Eight is essential, so that Year Nine teachers can complete the programmes of study and attainment record. The teachers from the two schools have had to work together very closely to make sure that Key Stage Three is properly organized.

As preparation for transferring to the upper school, some of the teachers from there have visited the middle school, to meet the children. The particular teacher Imtiaz met looked through his portfolio, talked to him about it, and asked to borrow examples of his work in various areas to show the teachers with whom he would start in September.

In the Upper School, Imtiaz joins a tutor group. All the tutor groups in Year Nine are timetabled at the same time for their PSE programme, which makes it quite flexible, and allows opportunity for the twice-a-year 20-minute review for each student to be spread over a period of time, during the PSE time. If the tutor wants to take a small group out for reviewing, the class is taken by another member of the team of tutors attached to that particular year group.

The upper school is keen to develop all the students' word-processing skills. When Imtiaz is in Year Ten and Eleven he is given opportunity and help to develop his own statement of achievement. In Year Ten this forms part of his report, and at Year Eleven he uses it to identify his targets for moving into the sixth form, and beyond. When the examinations are over in Year Eleven the school runs a 2-week induction programme into the Sixth form. Here, they get a realistic flavour of sixth form work and expectations. Throughout the upper school, increasing emphasis has been put on the students taking responsibility for their own learning, organizing their time, meeting course-work deadlines, planning their own next steps and making decisions about their futures. This induction programme is part of that process.

Other procedures continue too. Imtiaz is attached to a tutor, who does not assess the quality of what Imtiaz is doing in his Advanced Level ('A' level) classes, but encourages Imtiaz to make such judgements based on the regular feedback he gets from his subject teachers. The review collates and synthesizes evidence and records of his learning from both the school and outside. Imtiaz helps out regularly in his brother's shop at the weekend, and is learning a great deal about the way the business is organized. The review helps him to make connections between that learning and his economics course. Imtiaz is actually more expert than his tutor in this respect, but the tutor is able to prompt him to take his thinking further. As the choice of higher education comes closer, the tutorial time is spent making sure that Imtiaz knows where to look for the specialist advice he may need, and in preparing his UCCA and PCAS forms. Imtiaz is not surprised to learn that one of the Universities he is considering asks candidates to take their portfolio of achievement, with examples of their learning activities to date, with them to interview. The process of gathering this evidence, selecting and reviewing it has been part of his life at school for so long as he can remember, and it makes perfect sense for this to continue as his learning continues into Higher Education.

At 18 years of age, Imtiaz leaves home to start his higher education. He has been well prepared by his education experience so far to handle the independence he is now faced with. His teachers at school have encouraged him to be increasingly less dependent on them. When they first decided to encourage greater autonomy in their students by changing the way they worked with them, they worried about the possible impact on 'A' level grades that this might cause. They introduced new methods of working gradually, to allay their own anxieties as much as to help the students adjust and discovered, in fact, what some of them had believed — that the key to 'performance', academic as well as personal, lies with the motivation, organization and capacity for realistic self-monitoring of the students themselves.

Suggested Further Reading

BEECH, J.R. and HARDING, L. (Eds.) (1991) *Educational Assessment of the Primary School Child.* Windsor: NFER-NELSON.

BLACK, H.D. and BROADFOOT, P. (1982) *Keeping Track of Teaching: Assessment in the Modern Classroom.* London: Routledge.

DUNCAN, A. and DUNN, W. (1988) *What Primary Teachers Should Know About Assessment.* London: Hodder and Stoughton.

FRITH, D.S. and MACINTOSH, H.G. (1984). *A Teacher's Guide to Assessment.* Cheltenham: Stanley Thornes.

FREEMAN, E. and HARVEY, J. *Records of Achievement in Primary Schools.* London: School Examinations and Assessment Council.

GIPPS, C. (1990) *Assessment: A Teacher's Guide to the Issues.* London: Hodder and Stoughton.

MUNBY, S. *et al.* (1989) *Assessing and Recording Achievement.* Oxford: Blackwell.

RECORDS OF ACHIEVEMENT NATIONAL STEERING COMMITTEE (1989) *Records of Achievement.* London: Department of Education and Science and The Welsh Office.

SATTERLEY, D. (2nd Edition 1989) *Assessment in Schools.* Oxford: Blackwell.

SELKIRK, K. (ed) (1988) *Assessment at Sixteen.* London: Routledge.

SUMNER, R. (1991) *The Role of Assessment in Schools.* Windsor: NFER-NELSON.

TASK GROUP ON ASSESSMENT AND TESTING (1987) *National Curriculum: Task Group on Assessment and Testing.* London: Department of Education and Science and The Welsh Office.

TOWNSEND, S. (1982) *The Secret Diary of Adrian Mole Aged 13$\frac{3}{4}$* London: Methuen.

WATERHOUSE, P. (1990) *Flexible Learning.* Bath: Network Educational Press.

WATERHOUSE, P. (1989) *Supported Self-Study: An Introduction for Teachers.* London: National Council Education Technology.